EX·LIBRIS

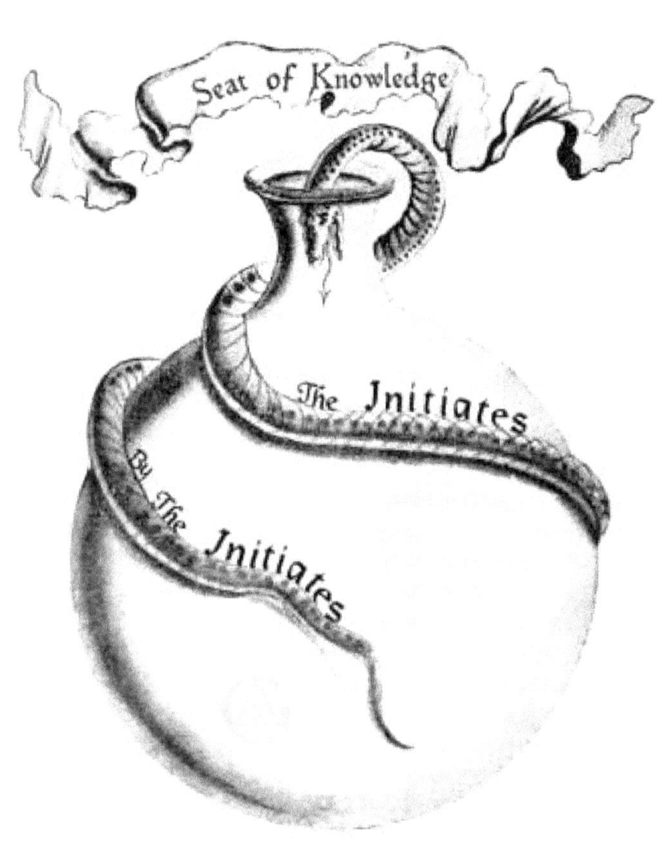
Seat of Knowledge
The Initiates
By The Initiates

The Initiates Speak
Book the Fourteenth

By: "The Initiates"

Compiled and Edited by
Darrell Jordan 32°

Production Editor
Yuka Jordan

Publisher
Seat of Knowledge

Made in the U.S.A.

But although all our knowledge begins with experience, it does not follow that it arises from experience. ~ Immanuel Kant

INTRODUCTION

The growing popularity of True Occultism and Mysticism throughout the whole world has at last induced us to try and issue a series, books that should be an honor to the Universal Father, to True Occultism and Mysticism, and to those who stand for all that is good in humanity. There is also another matter which has induced us to try to see whether such an effort would be appreciated.

This demand we will, therefore, meet, and "The Initiates" will be such a series of which every true student will be proud. We shall not, and will not, cater to that class of sensationalists who would make you believe that by studying a course in hypnotism, which they will sell you for a few dollars, you can be able to make men be your slaves or cause dollars to roll into your hands, for such things are impossible, and not only are they impossible, but it is this class of human ghouls who have brought down shame and disgrace upon a science which holds within itself all the religions ever known.

Not only does Mysticism hold within itself all religious teachings, but it holds the histories of such religions, and it can point the way from the lowest step upon the ladder up to the very highest, which is Imperial Initiation — the finding of the Christ. We shall stand for all that is pure and good in all religious beliefs. We shall try to give to our readers the truth concerning all religious beliefs and will at all times try to get the truth concerning all matters which concern our work. While on the one hand we shall not uphold anything, nor any one whom we know to be a fraud, yet it will not be our desire to tear down any system of thought, but rather to build up a pure and sublime system of philosophy, which shall appeal to the heart of mankind instead of to the mind, as so many do. It is not our desire to destroy, but to build up. Ours shall be an evolution and not a revolution. We believe that we are in a position to give to our readers that which none other can give them, for we are in touch with men and orders in every civilized country in the world, and we are in a position to obtain true facts concerning these matters from any part of the globe, and at short notice.

Regarding the orders of this series, we need only say that the true teachings, so far as they may be given to the profane world, will be given from time to time, and one of our greatest desires is that the old Egyptian religion may be explained in these pages, so that all men, and more especially all Christians, may know that the Egyptian priests did not teach idolatry, but that the people themselves, not understanding the greater mysteries taught, formed idol worship in spite of the teachings of the priests. These are but a few of the things that we shall hope to give to our readers, and all that we shall ask in return is that each and every one truly interested shall do all in his or her power to help and make this series a success. We all know that at the present age of commercialism nothing can be accomplished without the current coin of the realm. It will be our duty to do the work and obtain the material, but we must ask all those who have this great work at heart to do all in their power, so that we may receive the "sinews of war" wherewith to carry on the work, and if all will help in this we can assure each and every one that we will try to give them much more than they pay for.

The Initiates

THE GREATEST PROBLEM SOLVED

The problems that confront the world today are far too numerous to mention; but the solutions offered are many times as numerous; and they are as varied as they are numerous. The result is that the average person does not know what to do, either for himself or for society; therefore, he does nothing. He floats with the stream, and not only perpetuates, but intensifies those very conditions that the "lights" of the world are trying to remove.

Their work is for this reason mostly in vain, because no method for solving the problems of life will serve any purpose until the individual applies it in his own life. There is nothing gained in trying to lift up the masses unless each individual in the mass is taught how to lift up himself; and the effort of the few in trying to change the exterior conditions of the many, is love's labor lost.

Each individual must not only assist in changing his own conditions, but must take the leading part in bringing about that change. True, he needs the help of others to a degree; to a great degree if he has no training in the mastery of life; but to a slight degree only, if he has such training. However, the help he is to receive must be secondary to that which he is doing himself.

The very moment we try to help a person who depends more upon the efforts of his helpers than he does upon his own efforts, we are throwing our time and energies away; and nearly all the charity work, philanthropic work, and reform work done at the present time is of this kind.

It relieves for the time being, and is absolutely necessary as an aid to practical training in self-help; but alone it is utterly worthless as far as any permanent improvement is concerned. Why should we spend millions every year in taking people out of one pain and placing them directly into another?

Nevertheless, that is what we are doing in nearly all our present efforts to elevate the masses. These millions should be gradually turned into another channel, and employed in a system, the object of which should be to teach each individual to emancipate himself.

This system could be carried out on a larger and a larger scale, as its purpose and meaning became better understood; and in proportion to the increase of its work, the demands for charity and philanthropy would decrease. But to reach the individuals with this very wisdom of wisdoms will, to many minds, seems more difficult than any other "plan of salvation" that could be mentioned.

However, it is no more difficult to teach an individual to help himself than to teach him how to read; and any one in these days can learn to read. The real problem is to find a simple principle upon which to base such instruction; a principle that could reach every case; that all could understand, and that all could begin to apply in their present state of development.

Too many secrets to the new life are so abstract that only the highly educated can comprehend them; while the majority of the systems that could be helpful are so narrow that they appeal only to a limited number. They consequently fail to serve as a foundation for a worldwide movement that can and will emancipate the race. Those who are given to clear thinking know that every problem has a solution, and that the human mind is capable of finding that solution.

Therefore, the problem of problems can also be solved; and this problem is nothing more nor less than that of finding a method to emancipation and higher attainment that every individual can use where he now stands.

Every person, whether he be highly educated, or not educated at all, will agree that the following principle solves the problem under consideration: Be in Harmony with Everything, and Make the Best of Yourself. That is a principle that anyone can apply now, no matter what his mentality or environment may be; and whoever continues the application of this principle will reach the goal that he has in view.

When everybody is in harmony with everything, and when all are making the best of themselves, all the leading problems that now confront the world will disappear. Race problems, social problems, labor problems, financial problems, personal problems, domestic problems, national problems—all of these, and all of their kind will vanish of themselves.

The new problems that will come up during the progress of the race, each individual, or group of individuals can solve just as readily as the apt pupil masters his daily lessons in mathematics. But will the world in general take up this principle, and begin its immediate application? That, however, is not the question; the question is, can all minds begin to use this method where they stand now, and secure results from the very beginning?

We all must admit that they can; therefore, through the principle presented, the great problem is solved. That all could be induced to apply it at once, is not expected; but if those people who have the welfare of the race at heart, would base all their efforts upon this principle, and form practical movements, through which this principle could be presented directly to a constantly increasing number of individuals, more and more individuals would take it up voluntarily, and with enthusiasm, and it would not be long before the entire lump was leavened.

No matter where a person may stand today, he can begin today to place himself in better harmony with everything, and he can begin now to make a better use of the powers and qualities he may possess; and that he will help himself, advance himself, emancipate himself, and improve everything in his life by so doing, everybody knows.

All those who understand human nature to a degree, also know that there are thousands in every walk of life who would readily take up the application of this principle if it was properly brought before their attention.

Therefore, there is room for a movement—a world movement—with this great object in view; and the time is ripe for the immediate inauguration of such a movement. How this method is to be applied will depend upon the individual, because each one can use his own plan or system; it is only necessary that the two great essentials be constantly held in view—to be in harmony with everything, and to make the best of oneself. Whatever you meet, met that something in the spirit of harmony; and whatever you do, resolve to outdo all your previous efforts.

Whether you are appreciated or not must not concern you now. Your object is to be your best in every way; and after a little experience you will find that this is the secret to advancement, both in your work and in your life. How to make the best of yourself will be a question; but it depends upon how much of yourself you can understand now.

By applying the methods in self-development that you can master at present, you will soon be able to carry on your effort in this direction on a much larger scale. The better use you make of yourself, the more thoroughly will your mental development be promoted; and this will enable you to apply greater and more extensive methods as you advance. "To him that hath shall be given, and much gathers more."

Everybody has something to begin with; be it a few talents, character, physical strength, or simply life. Let him make the best use of what he now has, or is, and he will begin at once to advance. That it is necessary to be in harmony with everything and everybody is apparent to any mind at the very first thought; but the further we advance in the understanding of life, the more perfectly will we understand why harmony is necessary to the goal in view; and the more we shall gain from meeting everything in harmony.

However, both sides of the principle are at first so simple that anyone can understand them and apply them; but as any mind advances, both sides become more complex, and more extensive to supply the greater demands. Therefore, this principle will reach every case now, and will carry every individual onward as far as he may wish to go.

PSEUDO-MYSTICISM AND MODERN SCIENCE

Before we can substantiate a charge of false mysticism, we need to have some clear conception of true mysticism.

Essentially, mysticism is the conviction of an all-pervading and all-embracing One. The Universe is a universe. It is obvious that to all modes of intellectual cognition this conviction can only be a hypothesis. The act of knowing involves a separation, and an opposition, of the knower and the known; therefore of an all-pervading and all-embracing Unity there can be no intellectual knowledge. Intellectual knowledge excludes unity; unity excludes intellectual knowledge.

Mysticism not merely admits, but insists upon this. Unity is not known, but given in immediate experience; and this immediate experience of unity is known to have been such only when the experience itself is at an end. A unique and ineffable experience totally different from any kind of intellectual cognition, and given under conditions which definitely exclude any kind of intellectual cognition, is averred to be the self-experience of the all-pervading One.

This experience stands perfectly secure from all intellectual criticism. Intellectual criticism may legitimately apply itself to the intellectual interpretations of this experience; but with the experience itself it can make no contact.

It is clear that the conviction of an all-pervading Unity given in mystical experience is absolutely opposed to any form of religious or philosophical dualism. A real Unity cannot be half-hearted. Mind and matter, good and evil, may seem different enough in our practical lives, but the differences cannot be ultimate. They are differences necessarily established in the Unity by individual existences with the faculty of intellectual knowledge. Not that those who believe in the ultimate Unity of mysticism necessarily suppose that individual existence is a defect, though a nuance of this opinion is perceptible both in Platonism and

Buddhism. It is just as consonant with the convictions of mysticism to believe that individual existence is a necessary means towards the self-explication and self-consciousness of the One. In order that the One shall be conscious of itself it needs the individual mind, and it needs the development of the mind to the point at which it recognizes that its own inevitable intellectual perspectives are only perspectives. When a finite existence recognizes the conditions of its own existence, and a finite mind recognizes the conditions of its own operation, and these conditions are felt not as burdensome and oppressive, but merely as necessary, the pathway of the One into that individual existence is cleared of obstacles. The intellect has ceased to usurp a sovereignty to which it has no rightful claim.

Since Mysticism is irreconcilable with any Dualism, we have a short way of dealing with the assertions now frequently made by modern men of science that the modem scientific view of the world "leaves room for" Mysticism. Before being grateful for this condescension, we must inquire what kind of mysticism it is for which the modern scientist leaves room. If it is a dualistic mysticism, it is simply not mysticism; but an attempt to re-impose under that name the dualistic religion from which the Western mind is painfully struggling to free itself.

I cannot, in this brief space, permit myself the luxury of long quotations from such modern scientific apologists of 'mysticism' as Professors Eddington and Haldane. But it is true to say of both of them that the mysticism for which they wish to find room is a mysticism of 'values', or of 'morality'. "The real world," as Professor Haldane puts it, "is the spiritual world of values." Without discussing whether this statement is true, or whether it has any meaning, we can state quite peremptorily that this 'mysticism' is not mysticism at all. Mysticism knows nothing of "a spiritual world of values" as distinct from a "material world of facts."

The One of true mysticism is not the Good, or the True, or the Beautiful; it is the One. And in the One the Bad, the False, and the Ugly exist no less than the Good, the True, and the Beautiful. All alike, for true mysticism, are in some sense appearance. The goodness of the good thing is its element of appearance; because we call it good only in so far as, in some obvious or obscure manner, it promotes the fundamental propulsive energy of some individual human existences. And the badness of the bad thing is likewise its element of appearance. Their sheer existence alone is real.

True mysticism is beyond good and evil; and the mysticism which seeks to persuade itself or others that the One is good is a false mysticism. Mysticism does not seek to impose its personal terms upon the One. The One is not what we like, but that to which we and our likings belong. We cannot bargain with it, or propose conditions; and the true mystic has no desire to do so, That is what false mysticism finds it impossible to understand about true mysticism; for if it were possible for false mysticism to understand precisely that thing that, the true mystic has no desire that the One should be what he likes false mysticism would become true.

Mysticism, by whatever path it is attained, demands the stripping off of our personalities from ourselves. We surrender them, it is true, only to receive them again. But the personality we receive again, is not the personality we surrendered. It is no longer we who like, or think, or do, but the One which likes, or thinks, or does in us. And this impersonal personality we receive does not resemble the personal personality we surrendered. It is a new birth.

This impersonal personality can neither require, nor desire, that only the qualities it likes should qualify the One. The mere idea of such exclusiveness is strange, remote, fantastic. For the impersonal personality does not like things in the same way that the personal personality liked them. It is detached from them; it knows that its being does not depend on them; its affections towards them are disinterested. Therefore the desperate cry that what we love shall be eternal, and the desperate expedients by which some apparent answer to that cry is obtained, are alien to true mysticism.

In other words the validation of human ideals is no concern of true mysticism—with one great and momentous exception—the validation of the ideal of Unity itself. Mysticism claims that this ideal is real, and that it has direct experience of its reality. And precisely because this ideal is real, no other ideal can be real.

Now the 'mysticism' for which modem science, through the mouths of some of its chief expositors, seeks to make room is simply a mysticism devoted to the validation of human ideals. Since human ideals are never complete (or they would not be ideals), the validation for human ideals is merely the perpetuation of Dualism. The good is real, the bad is not; spirit is real, matter is not; the 'ought' is real, the 'is' is not. The arguments by which these preferences are deified are childish. It runs thus: Since the exact sciences do not give us a picture of reality, something else must. It is not certain; but even if it were, there is no ground at all for assuming that the moral preferences of a civilized European scientist supply the picture of reality which we need.

Not that those preferences are vain. The choice is not between their nullity and their omnipotence. This kind of dilemma which haunts the soul of 'religion' and 'science' alike is simply ignored by mysticism. Man's preference for the good, like everything else, is for the mystic a form taken by the One. It exists; and—this is the point—the man in whom it truly and strongly exists does not seek to have it validated. For him, and in him, it exists in its own right. The good would not be more desirable if it were proved to be the sole reality. "He who verily loves God," said

Spinoza, "cannot endeavor that God shall love him in return." The demand that human ideals shall be validated outside the human being, in whom they are real as his own right hand, is simply the endeavor "that God shall love him in return."

True mysticism does not need to have room made for it by science or any other mode of human knowledge. It occupies no room which they can occupy, for it does not exist in the same dimension. It is not an alternative, or a possibility. It is the simple truth underlying all existence. It is a certainty reached by the effort towards self-knowledge; it is simply the discovery that when the self is truly known, there is no self to know or to be known,—but only the One.

THE CONSTITUTION OF MATTER

WE read with interest in the New York Evening Journal an article entitled "Great Mysteries of Nature and Science" by the well-known scientist, Prof. Garrett P. Serviss, in which he says that "atoms are complex systems in which incomparably smaller particles are revolving around a center of gravity somewhat as the planets revolve around the sun" and that these atoms are "elastic, compressible, deformable entities, capable of yielding somewhat to every source of pressure which may be applied upon them." It is pleasing to have such words from the learned doctor, and more so that our University laboratories are aware of a fact known to Rosicrucian's for many long years.

Probably in years to come someone will discover the fact that the electrons are in similar relation to the atom as the atom is to the molecule. The diameter of an electron cannot be considered less than one ten-millionth part of an inch and probably even only one-tenth of that small dimension. The known kinds of elementary electrons differ in weight and heat capacity. They are always in motion, even when they form part of a "solid" mass, the rate of motion regulated by the specific gravity and temperature of the atom. If we consider that an atom of free hydrogen in ordinary temperature moves at the rate of one mile per second and performs about fifty thousand vibrations, we realize the impossibility of seeing the same, even if a microscope could be perfected to many times its present magnifying power. So even if we can prove some things we must judge the character of the atom by inference and theory.

This is the reason "science" is so slow to admit anything even though it has been forced to admit the existence of a "thought" and of "electricity."

Helmholtz holds the theory that the atom is simply a whorl in ether which pervades all space, and which must be supposed to be a perfectly elastic entity, like a jelly, though having no weight, and being in reality the only imponderable substance in nature. Would it be too much to expect science be able to understand that this ether consists of atoms of a lighter or more clarified material than that which we are used to work with?

This ether is the medium which transmits vibrations from the constituent particles of one mass to those of another. Sir Isaac Newton believed in the existence of some medium pervading space, but the formation of well-defined ideas in regard to its character dates from a later period.

Two or more atoms form a molecule, and probably this is the smallest division of matter of which we have the right to speak as though we knew something definite. The molecules of one element consisting of atoms differently grouped exhibit diverse properties, as oxygen and ozone, the diamond and charcoal. The molecules of different elements combine to form most of the substances with which we are familiar, from the combination of oxygen and hydrogen to form water up to some of the organic molecules which contain several hundred elementary molecules, while a few of the substances known to us, such as gold and silver, are simple elements.

The action of Nature may be defined as an incessant play of combination and dissociation, attraction and repulsion, between different molecules of different orders, with attendant results, and these changes involve variations of temperature and rate of vibration. It we consider that each electron and atom has its own limits of temperature outside of which it does not act, we draw the conclusion that the different sets of molecules are atoned to each other, as the musical vibrations for certain intervals of tone produce what is called harmony.

A PRODIGAL

SOMEWHERE I heard a story that almost parallels the story of the Prodigal Son with its beautiful lesson of Divine Providence, showing how the Father hath every soul in his loving care.

This young man, like many others, felt the lure of the big world beyond, and so he asked his father for the portion of goods that fell to his lot and started off on his long journey.

He left behind him the comforts of home, friends, and wise council, and made his way into a far country. But the father was a wise man and realizing that the son might come to want, secretly sewed some precious jewels into the folds of his robe, so that the young man might find them in the hour of need, when his substance was spent, and thus he enabled to return to his Father's house.

The young man wandered on, spending his substance in worldliness and vanity until his last farthing was gone, and he began to realize the meaning of want. Then he began to think and reason and compare. Hunger began to press upon him. He sought employment only to he turned away. Finally in this sore dilemma, almost beside himself, he began to pound his breast as people do in great trouble, as if they would pound nut of the soul a solution to their problem. In doing this his hand hit upon something hard in the folds of his garment, and searching to see what it could be, he found the hidden treasure, which enabled him to make his way back again to the shelter and guiding hand of a wise and loving father. It is a beautiful lesson of the way God provides and cares for us, and it only does faint justice, to the reality. It shows that the Divine Presence is ever with us, and in us, and the solution to every problem, the power to master, the wisdom and love to rise above every limitation is ever at hand. That Presence is ever with us no matter how far we may roam from its Kingdom of Love and Power.

In the story of the Prodigal Son we read that when the young man was returning and was still a great way off, the father saw him and ran and fell on his neck and kissed him. The father was watching for him and saw him while he was a far way off. This is a beautiful lesson, dear soul of Divine Mercy and goodness. Sometimes we do not learn our lessons in the light, and then darkness enfolds us, and out of the darkness we grope our way to the light and learn to appreciate the blessings that come in the light.

Note that in the state of mind the young man was in, the father could not help him. It was only as pain and darkness entered in that he began to look above or within for help, and turning his hack upon the transitory and the vain, he opened his being to the father's blessings.

Let us realize that "As our days so shall our strength he," and that no problem or difficulty can arise or confront us, but what Divine Love and Wisdom can solve, and no burden so great but the Great Burden Hearer can lift. No matter what our condition, there is always a remedy, always a Power superior to it that will respond through our faith, to our earnest appeal.

THOUGHT AND LOCOMOTION

WE often hear the expression, "How easy it will be for us to travel about in the ethereal realms when we lay aside our bodies. All we will need to do is to will to lie at a certain place, and we will be there immediately, even if our destination is a remote star." It is true that locomotion in the invisible realms is conducted with wonderful speed and under the direction of the will, but there are limitations that effect all beings move or less according to their state of development. For instance around this earth, and in fact around all heavenly bodies, are great magnetic or etheric zones that reach out one beyond the other millions of miles in space, becoming more intense in vibration as they graduate away from this earth. Earth-bound spirits, those who have passed from this plane with little or no aspiration, find themselves bound so close to earth conditions that they cannot rise into a higher altitude because of the intensity of the vibrations. They can only rise to higher planes as they spiritualize themselves, that is, purify themselves of all selfish and earthly dross. No one rises to a level higher than the plane he has attained to in spiritual progress. No one can rise higher than his vibratory force will carry him.

These magnetic or etheric fields have been separated into three great divisions called firmaments, the lower, middle and upper firmaments. Each of these are subdivided into three planes, the lower firmament embracing the first, second and third spiritual planes; the middle firmament the fourth, fifth and sixth spiritual planes, and the upper firmament the Divine or Celestial Realms. Paul, speaking of being taken to the third heaven, did not refer to the third spiritual plane, for that is not a high plane, but referred to the upper heaven or Celestial Kingdom.

"How that he was caught up into Paradise and heard unspeakable words, which it is not lawful (not possible with our limited faculties or means of communication) for man to utter." 2 Cor. 12:4.

To the lower firmament gravitate the souls who have not evolved or risen out of their mortal attachments or sense plane conditions. This is particularly true of those in the lower strata of this realm. In the higher slates of this realm they are awakening, and in the middle firmament are awakened to a greater degree of universal love and affection of the ego, and are more fully engaged in service to others. In the upper firmament, or realms of benediction and glory, reside the master souls, the great helpers and blessers of mankind. Only those who have cultivated a broad universal love and sympathy and mastered all mortal limitations, are qualified to enter this realm. Many of these great ones descend and work upon the lower planes, healing and teaching those less advanced. Many are able to work directly upon the earth plane when they can find souls who have elevated their vibrations through devotion and consecration, purity of thought and feeling, and by love and service, with their own high plane of thought and benevolent aims. With their greater vision, understanding and power they can deal with conditions from the invisible side of life that are hid from the eyes of their servants.

We look out into the blue sky, so symbolical of the infinity of Spirit, and a restful feeling steals over us, the effect of the soothing blue ray and the spiritualizing effect of looking up, which always opens up the petals of the soul to the spiritual light, and we wonder about the immensity of this deep, unfathomable ocean of blue, in which we can lose our cares and worries. Only when the stars come out at night do we realize that this ethereal vault contains something. Yet if we could see with added vision, or travel through its transparent waves, freed from our denser bodies, we would be surprised at the magnitude of life and activity manifesting everywhere, the Kingdoms, the

Societies, the Orders, the groupings of souls with allied interests, the institutions, the vistas of beauty and splendor.

One can project his thought immense distances and almost instantly make connection and communicate with another soul on some other planet or plane of life, providing of course he knows someone who can catch his call and respond to him, but to go there in person, that is, in your spiritual body, takes time. On this plane you can, or rather a few can, connect up immediately and communicate with others telepathically at a distance, even across continents and seas, but to go to them in person is a matter of days and sometimes weeks, according to the distance. This same law holds good in the spiritual realms.

"As above so below," or "As below so above." Although light in the more ethereal realms is made with wonderful rapidity, it is not instantaneous, for there are paths through space, and bars and obstacles to overcome, and detours to make, and a body cannot travel as fast as thought. There are suns and systems of suns so distant that it would take years and even centuries for a spirit to reach. We cannot with our limited faculties comprehend the vastness of God's universe. Some astronomer has said that when the telescope is stationary, the suns that pass through the field of the aperture look like an avalanche or a Niagara of falling stars.

A point of light in the heavens when viewed through the telescope is found to contain six thousand suns, all relatively as far apart as our sun is from the other suns near ns. New instruments applied in the measurements of stars have disclosed the great size of Betelgeuse (the great sun in Orion, in the shoulder of the great giant) which is so large that one-half of its bulk could not be squeezed between our earth and the sun which is 92,000,000 of miles away.

"When I consider thy Heavens, the work of thy fingers, the moon and the stars, which thou hast ordained: what is man that thou art mindful of him? And the son of man that thou visitest him? For thou hast made him a little lower than the angels, and hast crowned him with glory and honor. O Lord how excellent is thy name in all the earth."

WHAT EASTERN RELIGION HAS TO OFFER TO WESTERN CIVILIZATION

The decay of religious belief in the Western world is notorious, and I propose to take it for granted. There is now growing to maturity a generation of men and women to whom organized religion in the traditional sense of the word is meaningless. They do not subscribe to its dogmas with regard to the supernormal government of the universe, nor do they seriously endeavor to live the kind of life which it enjoins. Their skepticism is instinctive. It is not merely that the modern Western mind rejects this or that description of the supernormal world, or this or that explanation of the point and purpose of existence; it denies the existence of any world other than that which is known to the senses, and fails to recognize any purpose beyond the immediate purposes of daily life.

That this world is not in itself such as to satisfy our aspirations, or this life such as to invest the business of existence with significance, is unfortunately obvious. It follows that the modern Westerner tends to be cynical and indifferentist, and looking upon life as a pointless adventure in a meaningless universense, finds the rationale of existence in the satisfaction of his tastes and appetites. Where everything is uncertain, the doctrine of "let us eat and drink for tomorrow we die," at once concrete and definite, is eagerly embraced. The future being unknown, it is the part of wisdom to make the most of the present that we know. At the same time moral considerations, deprived of their supernormal backing, lose their accustomed force. God, we used to be told, takes delight in a good man. But once the practice of virtue is identified with pleasing God, it becomes difficult to ignore the respective consequences of His pleasure and His displeasure. Most religions have taken care to paint these consequences in the liveliest colors, with the result that it is difficult to say how much so-called virtuous conduct has been prompted by the desire to achieve an eternity of celestial bliss, and to avoid an eternity of infernal torments.

It is notorious today that heavenly rewards no longer attract and infernal punishments no longer deter with their pristine force; young people are frankly derisive of both, and, seeing no prospect of divine compensation in the next world for the wine and kisses that morality bids them eschew in this one, take more or less unanimously to the wine and kisses.

The resultant way of life is found less satisfactory than might have been expected. The objection to living for pleasure is that pleasure is so short-lived; repeat it and it no longer pleases. The objection to being able to do whatever you desire is that you quickly find that there is nothing that you desire to do. Hence the aimless and pointless character of much of modern Western life. We have revolted successfully against every kind of rule and authority, yet we are disillusioned with the results of revolt. We have shown the gods to be fictions, but we have still to come to terms with the needs that created the fictions.

In this impasse what assistance, if any, can we derive from the traditional wisdom of the East? Much provided the wisdom of the East be stripped of the religious dogmas which have accreted around it. Common to all religions is the belief that the universe is in some important and fundamental sense and, in spite of all appearances to the contrary, worthwhile. The appearances to the contrary include the everyday world and the everyday business of living in it. It follows that the everyday world is not the sole type of world; it may, indeed, be merely a mask or veil concealing a world of reality that underlies it. Further, it may be possible by living a certain kind of life to tear aside the mask and penetrate, however obscurely, behind the veil. Very well, then, it may be worthwhile to try to live the kind of life in question.

And here, I take it, we are within sight of the basic truth of all Eastern religions, which is that for those who live in a state of agitation, certain kinds of serene and lasting happiness, certain intellectual and creative processes, are impossible. Hence the religions of the East have insisted upon the systematic cultivation of mental quietness and the conscious pursuit of a certain way of life; in a word, they have laid down rules for the attainment of spiritual health.

Adopting them, we gain a criterion of value, a yardstick by which to measure and appraise the worth of our activities, which the current thought of the Western world fails to provide. Such a criterion of value invests our lives with significance by suggesting that it matters—and not only to ourselves—how they are lived. Given the belief that some kinds of activity are more valuable than others, we may go wrong, but we shall know that it is wrong, and that we might have gone right. Thus the belief in the intrinsic value of certain kinds of activity springs directly from the conviction of the fundamental worth-whileness of the universe. Lacking the latter, the Western world lacks necessarily the former. It has, in fact, lost the sense of value. Thus it prides itself continually on its ability to do things, without stopping to enquire whether the things are worth doing. Its boasted efficiency may indeed be denned as doing the wrong things in the right way. I take two examples.

No feature of Western civilization is more remarkable than the disparity between our mechanical skill and our social wisdom, between the powers we have won over nature, and the uses to which we put them. Science has given us powers fit for the gods and we bring to their use the mentality of schoolboys. Consider the mechanic by the roadside mending the carburetor of his car; in his knowledge of complex mechanism and in the skill with which he handles it, he is behaving like a superman. Consider the same mechanic ten minutes later, driving at forty miles an hour in a little hell of noise and dust and stench, unable to appreciate the country himself and precluding the appreciation of all who come near him; he is behaving like a congenital idiot.

Men of genius by the dozen, men of talent by the hundred have labored that wireless might be. They succeeded, and the tittle tattle of the divorce court and the racing stable is broadcasted to the remoter Pacific. In war time our medical science displays an almost incredible skill in patching up shattered bodies, in order that the equally incredible imbecility of our political science may set chemical science to work to blow them to bits again. In our scientific knowledge, we are gods; in our ethics and politics, quarrelsome babies. And the babies are entrusted with the powers appropriate to the gods.

What is the bearing of the wisdom of the East upon the situation? In the light of what has been said it is not far to seek. It consists simply in reminding the West of the fact that scientific knowledge and power over nature are of no value in themselves; their value depends upon the use to which they are put. If they are used to promote right living, they are good; if the contrary, harmful. It is necessary, therefore, first to discern what is right living. "You have taught us," said an Eastern philosopher to me, "to fly in the air like birds, and to swim in the sea like fishes. But how to live on the earth you do not yet know."

Or take the case of motion. The capacity for rapid motion is, as is well known, the brightest jewel in the crown of Western civilization. But one of the reasons why we move so rapidly from place to place is that we are not satisfied to remain in any place. We are driven by an aversion from the place in which we are, rather than an attraction for that at which we are not. This is particularly true of rich Americans, who, perpetually in transit across the Atlantic, seem to be running from something which is lying in wait for them on whichever side of it they happen to be. They suffer from a perpetually itching sole. This something is boredom, a boredom which springs from an inability to distinguish what things are really worthwhile, and an incapacity to pursue them.

Aware of the danger the East preaches the virtues of serenity and a quiet mind, as witness for example the following from an exposition of Taoism. "If a man desires too much or overworks and does not rest in time, the result will be the illness of Time..............The first step for a man who becomes a candidate for immortality is to keep life easy and the body young, since both mind and body have no inherent defect or trouble."

Speaking generally I should say that the Westerner tends to be discontented unless he has some positive reason for content; the Easterner, in so far as he has followed the teaching of his religion, tends to be contented unless he has some positive reason for discontent. The gift of contentment is, therefore, the chief gift which the East has to offer to the West, and this gift can only be received by those who have recovered the conviction of the fundamental worth-whileness of things.

THE CONSTRUCTIVE SIDE OF BUDDHISM

A well-known Buddhist philosopher of Tokyo recently warned his countrymen against the ever-growing tendency to look outside oneself for the means of gratifying one's desires or minimizing the sorrows of life. Now this tendency is not new in Japan, any more than in other countries, but obviously it has been accentuated by the introduction of Occidental civilization. Whereas in former times men were taught to resign themselves to the effects of their Karm a, many of us now-a-days think it at once our right and our duty to combat these evils as best we can, without seriously reflecting upon their causes. "Extinguish the flames of your own mind, and you will feel cool and refreshed in the midst of a great fire," says a Dhyana teacher. Not so a modern Japanese imbued with Western ideas. He has a scorn for those who apparently submit meekly to their fate. Science, he holds, has pointed out the way to the conquest of Nature. He shrinks from nothing in his endeavor to alter his surroundings to suit himself, but he remains ever dissatisfied with his lot. And no wonder, for in his eagerness to conquer the external world, he has forgotten how to control himself.

Now we may succeed to some extent in reducing the physical discomfort caused by climatic and other conditions. Medicine and sanitation may minimize disease and prolong life. Production may be increased and distribution equalized by efficient scientific methods; and it must be admitted that these improvements, or legitimate advances, in material civilization are to be welcomed, provided that they are calculated to liberate human energies for more enduring pursuits.

Buddhism has only too often been interpreted negatively and. has thereby been exposed to a charge of unfitness for an age of progress. It has been accused of pessimism and fatalism, love of passivity, and everything else unsuitable for an era of international competition. That the present state of social and international relations is far from desirable no one will dare to deny; and much good will certainly be done in the way of alleviating the fever of rivalry and jealousy if some of the "negative" teachings of Buddhism are put into practice. But it is not fair to insinuate that this religion is opposed to progress or science, or that it is essentially negative in its attitude towards life. I have already hinted at a more positive motive behind the Buddhist practice of almsgiving. Let me cite another instance, namely the negative form of the Buddhist commandments. The first of these runs: "You should not destroy life." Following this precept to the letter, you would be driven to the absurdity of refusing to use a vermicide. Disinfectants would have to be banned as involving the destruction of countless bacteria, the lowest forms of plant life. You would have to leave your fatherland at the mercy of an invading horde because resistance would mean war. Since even a vegetable diet requires the destruction of plant life, the logical outcome of following the inhibition slavishly to the letter would be slow and ignominious suicide. But self-destruction, whether by one's own hands or by passively falling a prey to starvation, disease and vermin, would be in itself a distinct violation of the great commandment.

No! This first Buddhist inhibition, like all the rest, is really positive and constructive in spirit. By the best Dhyana teachers in Japan it has been so interpreted, being paraphrased thus: "You should value life, both in yourself and in others." By deprecating the needless destruction of life, it implies in itself all the other inhibitions, for instance those against loose living, falsehood and slander, and the use and sale of alcoholic drinks. For these things constitute offences against life itself, and the injunction to value life in all sentient things amounts to an injunction to obey the highest laws of the universe. The Dharma or Dhamma, as these laws in their totality are called in Buddhism, comprises not only the natural laws with which modern science is chiefly concerned, but also the spiritual laws that are still above them and that obtain in all human relations. The injunctions and inhibitions of Buddhism derive their authority ultimately from the Dhamma, with which abstract Buddhahood itself is identified as the *Dharma-Kaya*. After centuries of internecine strife the leading Christian nations of the world are attempting to conclude a treat for permanent peace. Buddhism forestalled this anti-war declaration more than two thousand years ago by the very first of its commandments. And positively interpreted, this inhibition is the basis of all virtues—mercy piety, loyalty, friendship, charity, moderation, and even self-sacrifice,—for these can manifest themselves as occasion arises if only one knows how to value life in obedience to the highest spiritual laws. Furthermore, knowing the value of life does not necessarily involve the cowardly fear of death, since physical death sometimes becomes necessary to keep one's spiritual life inviolate. On the other hand, spiritual life may be ingloriously extinguished before the end of one's earthly career, or it may be kept alive and pure years after bodily death. Were proofs called for, let me cite here only three—Buddha, Christ, and Confucius, who are all more alive to-day than many a living priest, philosopher or moralist.

Returning now to the Buddhist teaching of self-conquest, which is the reverse of the modern

Occidental tendency towards self-assertion (the apparent cause of the present ascendancy of the white man), let me point out that this, also, is positive in the spirit. The European War has shown that the result of every nation aspiring to beat every other nation in armaments and commerce can only be mutual destruction. Thinkers in the West have come to realize the paramount importance of co-operation not only in social relationship but also among nations; and efficient co-operation can only be secured when each individual is willing to subordinate himself to the whole for the well-being of all. Self-conquest in Buddhism, be it remembered, does not mean self-abandonment or self-abasement. It means the suppression of the minor self for the liberation of the inner soul and the attainment of complete union or re-union with the Spirit of the Universe. Indeed, without this profound background—the Mysterious Essence of All Things—the principles of Buddhism, valuable as they certainly are as rules of daily conduct, would be commonplace in comparison with the esotericism of many another system of philosophy or ethics. Without the recognition, explicit or implied, of this Infinite Cause, all such Buddhas and Bodhisattvas as Amitabha ("Amida" in Japanese), Maha Vairocana

("Dainchi"), Avalokitesvara ("Kwannon"), and others so deeply adored by Japanese Buddhists would be in danger of descending to the level of mythological deities or idols. Only when recognized as symbolic incarnations or visible manifestations of the Infinite will they win the heartfelt veneration of the modern mind. But of this great subject, of the relation of the concrete to the abstract, of the symbol to what it symbolizes, of individual Buddhas to abstract Buddhahood, I may treat more at length in a future article.

THE PATH

The symbol of the Path has been used from time immemorial to suggest the never-ceasing, ever-progressing pageant of Life. Every expression of Life, from the soul of an atom to the Soul of a Sage appears to be slowly wending its way upon a road, the beginning and the end of which lie shrouded in darkness and mystery.

Many of these souls are being propelled along the Path of Evolution by the force of natural impulse, while other souls energize themselves. Some are blindly stumbling along the Path of Existence, while others are slowly and deliberately climbing the Path of Life. Some few Souls, having reached the summit of the weary road that "winds uphill all the way, yes to the very end," stand hesitant at the crossroad where the Path of Life divides. To the left a broad smooth highway stretches out, leading to liberation from all the woes of flesh; to the right a rugged, stony course, leading to renunciation of self for the sake of others.

The Path which the un-self-conscious souls are travelling lies far behind us; the Path of Initiation into the mysteries of Being lies far ahead. But the other roads lie at our very feet. Which shall we choose to travel? Shall we continue our stumbling way along the Path of Existence, caring little whence we have come or whither we are tending, or shall we boldly enter the Path of Life, armed with determination, humility and fortitude?

The old Chinese philosopher Kwang-Tze said of these two Paths: "There is the Tao (or Way) of Heaven, and there is the Tao of Man. These two are far apart and should be distinguished from each other."

The Path which so many of us seem content to travel is that in which the sensations and the feelings are allowed to dominate the life. But these are not the qualities which distinguish as men, for we share them in common with the brute. The line of distinction is marked by will, creative imagination, discrimination and the desire for altruistic service, and these powers must be exercised if we would assert our humanity and assume our divinity.

"Ye are gods!" thundered the voice of the old King-Psalmist; "I am verily the Supreme Brahman," asserted, in calmer accents, another ancient voice. These words of power, resounding through the halls of Time and reverberating down the centuries have been heeded by all whose hearts were tuned to their vibrations. In the golden days of Greece many listened to the ancient voices and reiterated their words. The Nous of Anaxagoras was but a restatement of the Hindu Brahman and the Egyptian *Nout*, and the philosophy of Pythagoras but a cadent echo of the voice of ancient *Aryavarta*. Socrates, meditating upon the import of these words, realized the divinity of his own nature and pointed the way of realization to other men. Plato and Plutarch hearkened and learned the nature of the Soul. We too must listen if we would fathom the depths of our own divine nature, for as Manu says: "Of all the duties, the principal one is to acquire the knowledge of the Supreme Soul; it is the first of all sciences, for it alone confers on man immortality."

The Path which leads to the "knowledge of the Supreme Soul" has been called by many names, and the way to reach the goal has been variously described. To each temperament one particular road seems most desirable, whether it be devotion, knowledge or self-sacrificing labor. But in the ancient Shu-King it is said that "We come by many branching roads and devious ways to the understanding of wisdom. I perceive that the forest trees are of many sorts and sizes, and those which bear fruit do not put it all forth upon a single branch."

This broad, unsectarian point of view is found wherever a true philosopher speaks. Only the cramped and limited soul narrows the world within the range of its own vision. The Path of Filial Duty, outlined by Confucius, is one of the many roads that leads to wisdom; the Path of Virtue and Purity so highly esteemed by Lao-tzu is another. We may choose between the several Paths described by Krishna in the *Bhagavad-Gita*, or we may tune the scale of our spiritual endeavors to the Buddhistic octave of right seeing, right willing, right speaking, right behaving, right living, right striving, right concentrating and right meditating.

We may turn, by temperamental affinity, to the poets, the philosophers or the moral instructors of the race in our search for spiritual guidance; we may look toward the "bloom of the East or the chambers of the West" for the Path which seems our own. But when our journeys are finished, we return whence we started to discover that the Path exists *within ourselves*, and that we—and none other—are the "way, the truth and the life."

The Path of Life is one in which every thought, word and deed is generated by the Pure Self within; therefore it is called the Path of Purity. When the flame of Pure Motive is applied to every action, the lower, instinctual self feels the pain of the burning, and the Path of Woe begins. But the Self can feel no pain; the sight of the pyre upon which the lower self is cast as a living sacrifice can bring but joy to the Self Supreme. And so the Path of Life becomes the Path of Bliss.

ALCHEMY

The exoteric historian rarely has sympathy with alchemy. He may reluctantly admit that modern chemistry is the legitimate off spring of alchemical researches, but for the most part he finds the Divine Art and Philosophical Wisdom an illusion, if not a willful deception. One of the greatest historians of chemistry, Hermann Kopp, epitomized his conclusions by saying that the history of alchemy is the history of an error. We may readily admit that, inasmuch as the theories of the alchemists are no longer useful in chemical science, they were certainly erroneous; but all scientific theories are necessarily only tentative and temporary. The modern critic, however, imputes to alchemy more than erroneous theories—he accuses it of inaccurate observation. The alleged transmutations, he avers, were either clever frauds, or the product was not genuine gold or silver, but an alloy unrecognizable by the imperfect methods of analysis then available. Possibly, again, unsuspected compounds of gold or silver may have been used in the materials upon which the supposed transmutation was attempted.

It is not our present purpose to discuss the perplexing question of the truth of the many well authenticated accounts of metallic transmutations carried out by the alchemists. We should, however, bear in mind that the present century has definitely witnessed the metamorphosis of one element into another, so that to transmute base metals into gold or silver cannot be declared completely impossible, even by orthodox chemistry. And there is every reason to believe that an ancient goldsmith was usually quite competent to decide whether a given metal was pure gold, an alloy of gold, or something of an entirely different nature. Archimedes difficulty with King Hiero's crown was to test it without damaging it; could a sample have been taken, any efficient contemporary goldsmith would have settled the problem with ease, by the ordinary technical methods.

Of more immediate interest is the undoubted fact that alchemy was more than a science, an art, or a craft: it was an esoteric system of wide comprehension and extraordinary continuity. It is, therefore, impossible to understand alchemy properly without a study of its possible origins, its underlying doctrines, and its inevitable and unbroken connection with mysticism. Even a brief survey of this vast subject would far exceed the limits of the present article, but certain features stand out in bold relief and force themselves upon our attention. First, perhaps, is the extreme antiquity of the alchemical tradition, which can be traced back through the centuries, from Europe to Islam, from Islam to Iran and Alexandria, from Greece perhaps to India and China, from Syria to ancient Egypt, Sumer and Akkad, Babylonia and Assyria—perchance even to the elusive Atlantis, though Plato's story may well have originated in hazy legends, transmitted from generation to generation, of Minoan Crete. The commonly accepted account, which would place the birth of alchemy in Ptolemaic Egypt, may possibly have misinterpreted the evidence and have mistaken for an origin *ab initio* what was merely a renaissance. In spite of all the patient investigation that has been carried out, we still know little of the beginnings of alchemy except that, far back as we may go, the art appears to be yet older.

Of equal interest with the antiquity and ubiquity of alchemical lore is the list of those who were known or supposed to cultivate it. Putting on one side such nebulous figures as

Hermes and Ostanes, we have still left an astonishingly large group of great men, many of them distinguished in other branches of human intellectual activity. Khazes, one of the founders of medicine; Avicenna, poet, philosopher and scientist; Jafar al-Sadiq, the Sixth Imam; Robert of Chester, one of the most versatile scholars of the twelfth century; Roger Bacon; Raymond Lully, missionary and mystic; Thomas Aquinas and his pupil Albertus Magnus; Khunrath, the obscure but accomplished German cabbalist; Robert Boyle, whose work in establishing the modern chemistry was of fundamental importance; and even the greatest of all men of science, Sir Isaac Newton. If alchemy were merely a piece of elaborate chicanery, would such a galaxy of intellects be found among its adepts or at least among those who thought sufficiently of it to study it with some persistence?

The truth seems to be that, while many were interested in the physical alchemy—such as Newton, whose duties as Master of the Mint obviously imposed upon him the duty of investigating the possibility of transmutation—others, perhaps the majority, were mainly concerned with the mystical system; for these, the synthesis of gold had little attraction. It is, however, to the occult side that attention must be turned if the true history of alchemy is ever to be written; too often an alchemical book has been dismissed as worthless by the historian because its chemistry is incomprehensible or erroneous, when perhaps its author had never intended it to be a treatise on chemistry but a manual of occult thought couched in the language of chemical symbolism.

It is possibly in this direction, too, that we may find an explanation of the persecution from which alchemists so frequently suffered. Those charlatans who defrauded men by passing off worthless alloys as pure gold doubtless brought alchemy into disrepute; but we may hesitate to accept such a cause as the sole one. A deeper reason seems to be the distrust which average public opinion always shows for the original thinker, for whom orthodoxy has no special sanctity. The sincere alchemists, in fact, appear often to have suffered ignominy because they were in the van of esoteric thought. The lives and writings of such men are worthy of respectful and sympathetic study.

WESTERN MYSTICISM

Compared to the East, the West is young. The past of which Western civilization is conscious reaches back a bare 2,500 years; and for nearly 2,000 of these the religion of the West has been Christianity. It is inevitable therefore that Western mysticism should, in the main, be Christian mysticism. But for those who, like the present writer, believe that mysticism is the essence of all forms of high religion, Christian mysticism is necessarily only a particular form of mysticism—a beautiful variety, no doubt, and one that has proved congenial to many of the finest spirits of the West. Without the Christian variety of mysticism the religious experience of the world would be definitely the poorer. The greatest poem of the Wrest would be unwritten.

There are three main sources of Christian mysticism, of which only two are generally recognized. The traditional account is that Christian mysticism derives from the contact, or confluence, of primitive Christianity with the mysticism of the Neo-Platonists, especially Plotinus. But this account is, I believe, only schematically or academically true. The most fruitful source of Christian mysticism is the mysticism of Jesus Christ himself. His teaching is the teaching of a mystic—of one of the world's greatest mystics. His doctrine of the Fatherhood of God, and of men's sonship to God, however much it may have been obscured by later theology, has remained the living core of Christianity. The first words of the central prayer of Christianity—Our Father: Pater Noster—contain for the true Christian the essence of his religion. If those words are more than an idle formula, if they express the reality of a genuine conviction, then they exclude as peremptorily as the rest of the teaching of Jesus excluded it, the subsequent theological dogma that He was the only Bon of God.

"No man knoweth the Father, but the Son" is, in fact, no claim of pre-eminence made by Jesus, but a simple statement of the prime fast of mystical experience the consubstantiality of man and God, which is revealed either immediately or not at all.

Into the beautiful detail of the mystical teaching of Jesus there is no space to enter in this brief essay; but the root of Christian mysticism is there and not elsewhere. The Christian mystic of the highest order (for example, Meister Eckhart of the fourteenth century) has always re-experienced the sayings of Jesus in their simple and obvious truth. He stands in the same immediate relation to God as Jesus himself once stood, and finds that the words of Jesus are naturally his own. To those words a true Christian mystic can make, as it were, authentic additions. Thus the great saying of Jesus to which I have referred: "No man knoweth the Father but the Son," on the lips of Meister Eckhart takes on a new beauty:

"The eye with which I see God is the same eye by which He seeth me."

"Mine eye and God's eye are one eye, and one sight, and one knowledge, and one love."

The mystical teaching of Jesus himself is the great source of Christian mysticism. But there is another. Christianity includes not only the teaching of Jesus, but his life and death. The contemplation of the life and death of Jesus is the distinctively Christian means to a mystical illumination. To watch the beauty and perfection of his life culminating in the agony of his death—to brood over what philosophy calls the problem of pain in all its nakedness—

has been for countless generations of true Christians the way to divine knowledge.

The sense that Jesus lives in spite of his disaster, and more potently because of his disaster, is the spiritual justification of the belief in his bodily resurrection which is the central dogmatic belief of Christianity.

Christ is thus eternally resurrected in the truly Christian soul. This experience is the foundation of the mystical Christianity of St. Paul; it is equally implicit in the famous "spiritual exercises" of St. Ignatius Loyola, the founder of the Jesuits,—exercises which are still the basis of Jesuit discipline; it may be found in the beautiful words of one of the greatest of English Christians—Bishop Lancelot Andrewes:

Look upon him till he look back upon us again. For so he will. And if we ask, how shall we know when Christ doth respect us? Then truly, when fixing both the eyes of our meditation upon him that was pierced—as it were with one eye upon the grief, the other upon the love wherewith he was pierced, we find by both, or one of these, some motion of grace arise in our hearts, the consideration of his grief piercing our hearts with sorrow, the consideration of his love piercing our hearts with mutual love again. These have been felt at this looking on, and these will be felt, it may be at the first, imperfectly, but after with deeper impression; and that of some, with such as none knoweth but he that hath felt them.

The mysticism of Christ, and the mysticism of Christianity are different. But they are not altogether incompatible; and it is probable that no man can truly experience the latter, unless he has a glimpse into the former, because no man can understand the perfection of the love of Christ, except by understanding his teaching.

These then are the two main sources of distinctively Christian mysticism. Unless these are clearly recognized and distinguished, there is a danger of over-estimating the importance of the third source—the Greek mysticism which enters Christianity chiefly through "Dionysius the Areopagite" (who was probably a Syrian monk of the 5th century) and which reached him through Plotinus from Plato. What came into Christianity from this source was not so much mysticism itself, of which, as we have seen, there was abundance in Christianity from the earliest times, as a philosophy of mysticism—a theory and technique of mystical experience in which there is nothing distinctively Christian. We meet it early in the Christian father, Clement of Alexandria, who in his "Stromata" thus describes the attainment of the knowledge of God.

Going forth by analysis to the First Intelligence, taking away depth, breadth, length, and position, leaving a monad, then abstracting all that is material, if we cast ourselves into the vastness of Christ, thence if we proceed forward by holiness into His Immensity, we may in some fashion enter into the knowledge of the Almighty, recognizing not what he is, but what he is not.

Here is clearly formulated, as early as the third century, the *via negationis*, which is familiar to philosophical mysticism throughout the world. Clement of Alexandria was the teacher of Origen, who maintained the reality and the necessity of an esoteric religion, and supported his contention with an appeal to the example of the Persians and the Indians. Of Clement of Alexandria, and still more certainly of Origen, it may be said that they were clearly conscious that Christianity was merely a variety of a universal, esoteric and mystical religion. They join hands, quite naturally, across a space of fifteen hundred years, with the English poet, John Keats, who after describing the world as "a vale of Soul-making," continues:

Seriously, I think it probable that this system of Soul-making may have been the Parent of all the more palpable and personal schemes of redemption among the Zoroastrians, the Christians, and the Hindoos. For as one part of the human species must have their carved Jupiter, so another part must have the palpable and named Mediator and Saviour, their Christ, their Oromanes, and their Vishnu.

Probably the great contribution of Greek Neo-Platonism to Christian mysticism was the awakening of the sense, in those who received it, of the reality of a universal religion, and of Christianity as one form, among many, of this universal religion. How inevitable this was we may see by considering a single utterance of "Dionysius the Areopagite," who more than any other single mystical writer influenced Christian mysticism during its greatest period—the thirteenth and fourteenth centuries:

And thou, my dear Timothy, in thy intent practice of the mystical contemplations, leave behind both thy senses and thy intellectual operations, and all things which are known by sense and intellect, and all things which are not and which are, and dispose thyself as far as may be to unite thyself in unknowing with him who is above all being and all knowledge, for by being purely free and absolute, out of self and out of all things, thou shalt be led up to the ray of the divine darkness, stripped of all and loosed of all.

"Dionysius" was a Christian monk; but there is nothing specifically Christian in this fine passage. Yet for the mediaeval Christian mystic the writings of "Dionysius"—and this passage in particular—possessed an authority equal to that of the Scriptures themselves.

Meister Eckhart was steeped in his writings: he quotes "Saint Dionysius" with the same reverence as the Fourth Gospel: and in Eckhart we find the most perfect harmony of the various elements which went to compose Christian mysticism. His use of the distinctive and hallowed phrases of Christian piety is constant, but never forced. If he uses them in new ways, we are conscious that he thereby penetrates to the depth of their spiritual meaning. For Eckhart, God's begetting of his Son is an eternal act, perpetually renewed in the human soul. Indeed, the attainment of his soul by the individual man is, for Eckhart, really identical with the begetting of his Son by God in man. As he puts in it in one of his most memorable phrases: "He who abides always in a present Now, in him doth God beget his Son unceasingly." It would be almost an impiety to attempt to wring the meaning from a phrase so pregnant. We may content ourselves with pointing out how closely it links the highest Christian mysticism with the later mysticism of Goethe. Here is Goethe's doctrine of "the eternality of the moment," at which he labored so hard to arrive—"the eternal moment" in which the finite existence becomes the pure instrument of that being which is beyond existence.

One might accumulate quotation upon quotation to show the richness and universality of Christian mysticism. "There is a force in the soul," says Eckhart again, "and not only a force, but something more; it is so pure, and high, and noble in itself that no creature can come there, and God alone can dwell there. Yea, verily, and even God cannot come there with a form; he can only come with his simple divine nature." Yet again,

How are we God's sons? By having one nature with Him. But any realization of this, of being God's sons, is subjective, not objective knowledge. The inner consciousness strikes down to the very essence of the soul. Not that it is the soul itself, but it is rooted there and is in a measure the life of the soul, her intellectual life, the life, that is, wherein a man is born God's son, born into the eternal life, for this knowledge is a-temporal, unextended, without here and without now. In this life all things are the same things and all things common; all things are all in all, and all atoned.

One is not surprised that Eckhart, the purest, the subtlest, and the simplest of all the great Christian mystics was condemned (though after his death) for heresy. In such a doctrine as his there was manifestly no place for a Christ who was "the only-begotten son of God." "I maintain," he said roundly, "that we can no more be wise without wisdom than Son without the filial nature of God's Son: without having the very same nature as the Son of God himself." Such doctrine is impossible, and intolerable, to Christian orthodoxy. But there can be little doubt in the mind of any patient student of his sayings that it was the veritable doctrine of Jesus himself. The "good tidings" that he preached in Galilee were that it was possible, and necessary, for any and every man to know that he was the son of (or consubstantial with) God, by precisely the same way and with precisely the same certainty that Jesus himself had attained the knowledge that he was the son of (or consubstantial with) God.

This immediate experience of the truth of Christ's teaching which Eckhart evidently possessed, returns again and again in the history of Christian mysticism; and, naturally, it is in continual danger of being repudiated by the church. The possibility of harmonizing it with any rigorous form of Christian orthodoxy is always slender. No doubt, the doctrine of "the indwelling Christ" is theoretically legitimate; but the limitations imposed upon it are such that a great Christian mystic must always override them. For the Christian mystic it is obviously inevitable that Christ must occupy a position like that which is occupied by the Buddha; he is one of the greatest, to a Western mind perhaps the greatest among the greatest, teachers of religion; but his relation to God was no closer than that which it lies within any man's power to attain, provided he possesses the power, and the will, and the love. Thus Christian mysticism gnaws continually at the root of Christian orthodoxy.

It is probably to this cause that we must attribute the striking fact that since the seventeenth century, when the full effects of the Renaissance and the Reformation were felt, there has been a manifest decline of specifically Christian mysticism. At first, it found refuge in the Protestant sects, among whom the Quakers, at least with their doctrine of "the inner light" were true mystics. But the purest expression of Western mysticism was no longer in any form of Christianity. It passed henceforward into the work of the poets and the philosophers. Spinoza, Novalis, Goethe; the great succession of English "romantic" poets, Wordsworth, Coleridge, Blake, Keats, and Shelley; and today, the many "prophet-teachers" in rebellion against the painfully inadequate doctrine of scientific materialism which dominated the nineteenth century—in these the tradition of Western mysticism is perpetuated.

But its forms are infinitely various. Whether that multiformity is the weakness or the strength of modern mysticism the future must decide. There are many who look back wistfully to the time when Catholic Christianity was truly the universal religion of the West, and when it accommodated within itself (though with some visible strain) a highly developed mysticism, I do not share these longings for the past, though I can sympathize with them. I believe that the future of religion in the West lies with a Christianity that is perfectly conscious of itself as one among many forms, one among many idioms, of a universal religious knowledge. Such a Christianity will, manifestly, no longer be Christianity, which has always made for itself the fundamental claim that it is a unique and final revelation of the nature of God. There are very few, even among professed Christians, outside the Roman Catholic Church, who believe this in the West today. And perhaps the time is not far distant when those who feel within themselves the truth and necessity of religion, but are still afraid to leave hold of their institutions and their exclusive creeds, will have learnt the truth (and found the courage to proclaim it) that was boldly uttered by Meister Eckhart, six hundred years ago:

He who seeks God under settled forms lays hold of the form while missing the God concealed in it. But he who seeks God in no special guise lays hold of Him as he is in Himself, and such a one lives with the Son, and is the Life itself. We might question life for a thousand years; 'Why dost thou live?' It would only say, if it replied at all, 'I live because I live.' For life lives in a ground of its own, wells up out of its own. It lives without a cause, for it lives itself. And if any one asked a proper man, one who works his own ground. Why dost thou work?' he too would say if he told the truth: 'I work because I work.'

THE TEACHING OF REBIRTH IN INDIA

"If I were asked to describe the western world," Schopenhauer reported to have said, "I should have to say that it is the benighted region where the idea of rebirth is unknown."

True enough, perhaps, in his day, this is now altogether false; for the western world has caught the idea of rebirth with marvelous quickness spreading it far and wide, as on electric nerves; absorbing it, dissolving it in thought, putting it forth under new lights; so that very soon the time will come when any mind not receptive of this idea will be of interest wholly archaeological.

Coming to us from the East, through eastern messengers, the idea of rebirth will one day be made our own—altogether ours; then it will wear a new face vivified by our new, strong life, and expressing that new Spirit in us which no other race or nation ever had,—the new Spirit, latest birth of endless being, that is our warrant for separate existence.

But at present, and for a long time yet, the idea of rebirth must remind us of the East, carry us back to the East, and the long past ages and races that have left us our earliest records of the eternity of life—life eternally changing, eternally one. And indeed everyone in dwelling on the idea of rebirth, has thought of the East and spoken of the East very abundantly, often eloquently. Yet, after all this eloquence, there is still a great need that someone should try, earnestly and with knowledge, to find out and record precisely what the Eastern teaching is; neither blinded to grand old truths through lack of sympathy; nor, through excess of enthusiasm, tinging them with new life of our own. To do this for Chaldea and Egypt will soon be possible, though not completely possible yet; to do it for India is not only possible, but comparatively easy, for we have abundant records, we know their meaning fairly well, and even their relative age, though we can as yet only guess at their age in years. Here, then—as far as our best knowledge goes—is the oldest passage in all the vast records of India that speaks quite clearly of rebirth. It has a historical atmosphere of the greatest value, to the significance of which we shall presently recur. We are told, in this very ancient passage, that a young Brahman, the son of priestly ancestors, came to the gathering of the Panchala nation, to the court of King Pravahana son of Jivala, the seer and sovereign of the Panchalas. The King, seeing the young Brahman, greeted him; then asked him whether his priestly father had handed on to him the traditional sacred teaching. The youth, Shvetaketu, proud in his Brahmanical knowledge, replied with a simple affirmative, which was the sacred syllable, probably the password of initiation.

Then the royal sage asked him five questions, deep and searching, not at all touching the lesser mysteries of the sacrificial rites, but concerned with the profound realities of life: "Do you know how these beings, ongoing forth from life, separate, and pass on in diverging ways? Do you know how they come back to this world again? Do you know how the other world is not filled to overflowing by the multitudes that ever go forth from life? Do you know after the offering, of what offering the waters, taking human voice, rise up together and speak? Do you know the approach of the path of the gods and the path of the fathers,—or, through doing what, men approach the path of the gods or the path of the fathers?"

The confident affirmation of the young Brahman, proud in priestly knowledge, turned to as brief a negative—a negative five times repeated, we may guess, with growing bitterness and confusion, but not, the old record tells us, with growing humility. For when the kingly sage, gently rebuking his ignorant assurance, offered to teach him the more excellent wisdom, the young Brahman, quaintly says the text, "ran away." Coming home to his father, he said bitter things of the king, told about the five questions, and reproached the old priest for not handing on to him the whole teaching, thus letting his vanity be wounded by one of the kingly race. We cannot but admire his father's answer: "You know us, dear,—how, if I was learned in anything I told it all to you; but let us go to the kingly sage and become his pupils."

But Shvetaketu had had enough of the Panchalas and their lord, and told his father to go himself. So the old Brahman went alone to ask for wisdom. The king received him well, and hospitably entertained him; then after the manner of the "tempter" in all allegories of initiation, offered him a wish. The old man rejected the things his fellow Brahmans prayed for—"Enough of gold and cattle and horses, slave-girls, tapestries and robes! But be not ungenerous of the great, the endless, the everlasting."

The king's answer to this prayer for wisdom is remarkable—almost startling. He consents to teach the old man the way of rebirth and of freedom from rebirth, but adds this notable caution: "Henceforth be free of offence towards us, thou and thy father's fathers, since this wisdom never before dwelt in any Brahman, but was, in all lands, the mastery of the warrior Kshattriya, alone."

Here then, at the very outset, in the very first passage where the teaching of rebirth occurs, we are quite distinctly told that this teaching was then utterly unknown to the Brahmans, though versed in the Vedic hymns; that, on the other hand, it was handed down as a mystery-teaching among the Kshattriya or Rajputs, the warrior race that ruled the whole of northern India. To this remarkable tradition, which all the subsequent ages of Brahmanical tradition have not been able to efface, we shall return later.

This history of the king of the Panchalas,—a race whose descendants are almost certainly found in the Rajput warriors of today and whose ancestors were called Rajputs as far back as the Vedic age, comes down to us by three distinct channels, one of which is evidently independent of the other two. The two closely related versions are in the Brhad-Aranyaka Upanishad and the Shatapatha Brahma,—of which the Upanishad in question now forms a part. An independent Version of the same story is in the Chhandogya Upanishadi, so that the two greatest and most important Upanishads, or Indian books of hidden wisdom, endorse and record the same historical fact—that the Brahmans first learned the teaching of rebirth from the Rajputs; and this in connection with the earliest passage, as far as our best knowledge goes, in which the teaching of rebirth occurs.

This very remarkable conclusion has never before been stated in so many words; yet it would be quite easy to shew that all the best Vedic scholars have been feeling their way in the same direction. It this teaching were taken away, the heart of Indian wisdom would be lost; and yet this crown of "Brahmanical" philosophy, as it is called, belonged not to the Brahmans at all, but to the Rajputs, the warrior-Kshattriyas, from whom the Brahmans learned it, humbly sitting at their feet.

In the Chhandogya Upanishad, the old Brahmanwho first learnt this doctrine has put it on record that his son Shvetaketuwas "conceited, vain of his learning, and proud; we may add to this unprejudiced paternal judgment, that Shvetaketu, though he knew the three Vedas by heart, must also have been uncommonly stupid and unobservant; for had he but listened closely to what the Rajput sage asked him, he might have guessed the answers; if ever there were leading questions, these are. Let us supply the young Brahman's short-comings, and tum the five questions into affirmations: These beings, the souls of men, ongoing forth from life, are separated and go onward in divergent directions; souls come back to this world and enter it again; and because the souls of men come back to this world again, the other world is not filled to overflowing; but the souls of men do not immediately come back to re-enter this world, for we hear of two paths, not of this world, that they approach, in the way of the fathers and the way of the gods. It must be at the dividing of these two ways that they separate and pass on in divergent directions—some to the fathers, the souls of dead ancestors; some to the gods, the shining immortals.

Here then, in the questions themselves we have a perfectly clear picture of the teaching that was in the Rajput sage's mind; if we had nothing but these questions, no answers nor anything else in all the Upanishads, we should yet have a lucid outline of the doctrine, enough to serve as a clue to the mystery of death. But we have his answers fully recorded, and much more of the same teaching in other parts of the same and other Upanishads; and these teachings, when brought together, enable us to fill in the outline with wonderful richness and completeness. To begin with the Rajput sage's answers.

In order to insist on the interdependence of immortality onwards and immortality backwards, the thing begins, not, as we should expect, with the moment of death, but with the period before birth when the soul is getting ready to enter the world. In the great All, he teaches, there are three manifested worlds; the divine, the mid-world, and this earth.

The divine is as a fire that illumines; the mid-world of passion is as a fire that consumes; this wholesome earth is as a fire that warms. The soul that is to enter the gates of birth is resting in the divine world; how it came there, we shall shortly see. When the time of birth comes near, it dies out of the divine world, to be born into the world below, the world of passion and desire, the midway between earth and heaven.

When the soul dies out of the celestial world, it is reborn in the mid-world in a lunar form; that is, a form of waxing and waning, of changefulness and desire that is likened to a white mist gradually darkening to cloud. Then it gradually takes on the materiality of the earth and approaches a father and mother to be born.

The three worlds were likened to three fires; the same image is applied to the father and mother; so that after the offering of the fifth fire, after the mother has given birth to her child, "the waters"—the gradually materialized form already likened to a mist condensing into cloud—"rise up and speak with human voice" the voice of the new-born man. His fate in this solid-seeming world is described with striking brevity; "he is born, he lives as long as he lives, then dies.''

No epitaph could be briefer; the driest human record would give more facts than this. But the Rajput seer deals thus summarily with the facts of life because he wishes to pass on the more swiftly to the weightier facts of death. After death, the soul rises up from the pyre, "reborn, of the color of the sun; then comes the dividing of the ways.

Those who have lived in pure spirituality, shining intuition, spotless truth, pass onward along a luminous path through shining worlds to the divine sun, the Self of all beings, the perfect Eternal.

"For them there is no return they go not out any more. For the others, those who sought not the inner spirit but the outward forms of things, praying for "gold and cattle and horses, slave-girls, tapestries and robes," worshipping through rites and ceremonies, "sacrifices and pious gifts," "approaching God like a cow to be milked," hoping to win, not God but the gifts of God, in this world and the next—for these there is a lower way.

They enter paradise, the "lunar world," where all things are reflections, not realities, as the moon reflects the light of the sun. Here "in the world of good works they enjoy bliss in the upper half of the life-circle" in the words of another Upanishad." The Rajput sage, in speaking of the paradise of reward, uses a strange expression which he does not fully explain. The souls of men, he says,—that is, their life-experience—become "the food of the bright powers" in paradise."

To understand what this means, we must tum to another passage of the same Upanishad—a passage full of magnificent color and beauty, where the life of the paradise of reward is made conceivable by the analogy of dreams.

This passage teaches that the great reality is the Self, "the inner light in the heart, consciousness, spirit;" that the Self ever remains the same, though it seems to enter both worlds, as if thinking, as if moving.

When the man falls asleep, the Self transcends this world, transcends the forms of things that die. For when at birth man enters into a body, he is enwrapped and involved in perishable things, but ascending again when he dies he puts off evil things.

For there are two dwelling places for the spirit of man; this world and the other world. And the world uniting these two is the dream-world. And when he is in the world that joins the other two, the spirit of man beholds both this world and the other world. And according to what he has attained in the other world, coming to that attainment he beholds things perishable or things blissful. When he "falls asleep," taking his materials from this all-containing world, himself having cut the wood, himself the builder, by his own shining, by his own light—when he thus "falls asleep" he is his own light.

There are no chariots there, nor horses, nor roads; so he himself puts forth chariots and horses and roads. There are no joys, rejoicings, nor enjoyments there; so he himself puts forth joys, rejoicings, enjoyments. There are no Springs or streams or lakes there; so he himself puts forth springs and streams and lakes. For he is the maker, the creator.

This is as close a rendering of the original Sanskrit as the greatest care can make it. In the answers of the Rajput seer, and in one of the questions, the Symbols are required to be interpreted in the light of other passages; but here are no Symbols—only the most lucid and vivid teaching, the like of which we might seek in vain elsewhere, throughout all the books in the world.

The teaching is this: Life after death, for those who are to be born again, is a bright and radiant dream; a fairy palace, of which each one is the builder, "himself having cut the wood;" and just as in dream "things seen as seen he beholds again, things heard as heard he hears again, and what was enjoyed by the other powers he enjoys again by the other powers; things seen and unseen, heard and unheard, enjoyed and un-enjoyed, real and unreal,—he sees all, as all he sees it."

The magician in paradise, as in dream, is the spirit, working through the Creative, formative imagination; the magician's materials are drawn from the experiences of this all-containing world.

"According to his spiritual attainment,"—to use the excellent phrase of the Upanishad,—according to the measure of his aspirations is the scenery of his paradise; if his spiritual unfolding was meagre, he will be surrounded by sensuous delights; if richer and higher, he will rise above them, "going back to the higher divinity."

All his spiritual aspirations, all the divine movements of his life, where he has risen above the perishable longings of the perishable world, to something higher, holier, more real; every act of gentle charity, high heroism, self-forgetfulness,—this is his "attainment in the other world" his spiritual earnings, his treasure laid up in heaven.

These fair aspirations and intuitions are forces, the most potent forces in the world; they are quite strictly guided by the law of Conservation; quite strictly work themselves out to their fullest fruition.

In dream, it is exactly the same; as a man's imaginings, so are his dreams—for the sensual, sensual; for the pure, pure. And those whose aspirations are high and shining, do really reach a higher world, and come back to waking life radiant with alight that never was on land or sea.

After sleep comes waking. The shining aspirations and intuitions have reached their fullest unfolding and fruition. The shining powers of the spirit have feasted on the spirit's experience; the man is ready to be born again. "Therefore he whose radiance has become quiescent is reborn, through the impulses indwelling in mind." Here is the second great truth bound up in the teaching of rebirth: the man's soul comes back, not fortuitously, but quite strictly guided by forces of his own making; his new life is as much his own work as was his paradise. He is reborn by law, not by luck.

This truth is covered in an admirable series of similes in the great Upanishad from which we have quoted so much already: "What a man has known,—we are told,—what he has done, and the insight he has already gained, take him by the hand.

Then, just as a Caterpillar, coming to the end of a blade of grass, lays hold on another and lifts himself over to it, so this Self, after leaving aside the body and putting off the perishable things of this world, lays hold on his attainment and lifts himself over to it.

"And, just as a goldsmith, taking the gold of one fair work, makes of it another new and fairer form, so this Self, after laying aside the body and putting off the perishable things of this world, makes for itself another new and fairer form, like the form of the souls, of the celestial singers, or the gods or the lord of beings, or even the great Evolver, or some other form." "According as a man has walked and worked, he comes to being; he who has worked highly, comes to lofty being; he who has worked evil, comes to evil being; through holy works he comes to holy being, through evil to evil."

For they say indeed that "the Spirit is formed of desire; and according to his desire, is his will; and according to his will, are his works; and whatever works he works, to that he gives." As the verse says "he, enmeshed by his works, goes to whatever form he has intended his mind on."

And after gaining the reward of his work, of whatever he has worked here, he returns again from the other world to this world of work. In the answers of the Rajput sage, the return to rebirth is described in the same words as the first birth of the soul, with which his teaching opens.

After telling how their experiences become the food of the bright powers in a paradise that has its waxing and its waning, he teaches that, when their life-cycle there is fully run, they descend again, through spheres less and less ethereal, toward the earth, "are sacrificed once more in the fire of man, again born in the fire of woman, and come forth again into the world.

Thus, verily, they go on along their cyclic course." The version of the Chhandogya Upanishad runs more to precise detail; thus, for instance, when birth is spoken of at the beginning of the Rajput's teaching, we are told that the man to be born "wrapped in the womb, lies there as an embryo, and is born at the end of the tenth lunar month, or as long as it may be."

The same instinct for detail appears when the causes of rebirth are spoken of. We are told that "having dwelt in paradise according to the length of their treasure, their accumulation of aspiration, they return again by the same road. They become ethereal, then breath-like, then smoke-like, then vaporous, then cloudy, descending like rain toward the earth.

Then for those whose walk in life was happy, there is the prospect of a happy birth, as a knower of holy things, or a warrior or a man of wealth; but for those whose walk in life was foul, there is the prospect of a foul birth, dog-like or swinish or outcast. But these mean creatures, who are perpetually returning, for whom it is "be born, die!"—they go by neither of these two paths. This is the third way—beware of it!

As the verse says: "the stealer of gold, the drinker of spirits, he who dishonors his teacher's household, he who slays the saints—these four fall; and fifthly he who walks with them!

This last teaching is logically necessary to complete the whole. There are three alternatives. Those who at death have spiritual attainment, only, no earthward impulses indwelling in mind, and cannot be drawn back to the earth; all their tendencies are spiritwards, so they themselves go spiritwards along the path of freedom, to the perfect oneness with the Eternal.

Those who have a "treasure in heaven," a spiritual attainment, an "accumulation" of moral force, aspiration, intuition, and, side by side with this, have also earthly impulses indwelling in mind, are prevented by these earthly impulses from reaching perfect freedom; yet they cannot be prevented from enjoying their spiritual attainment to the full; they reap their perfect reward in paradise, dwelling there as long as their accumulation lasts. Then the earthly impulses re-assert themselves, their higher radiance has become quiescent, and they are re-born through the tendencies indwelling in mind.

But those who have no "spiritual attainment," no "accumulation" at all; who have only earthly impulses and nothing else, cannot enter the reward of paradise, much less the path of liberation. The earthly impulses reassert themselves immediately, unchecked, and they are at once reborn.

To show that this interpretation of the threefold alternative is no gloss on the old mystery-teaching of India, we may add here the same doctrine in a slightly different vesture, from another of the Upanishads. A word or two as to the Symbols used in this slightly veiled teaching.

The mystic syllable, which represents the Eternal, the All,—conceived as unconditioned or conditioned, as higher and lower,—is divided into three measures which stand for the three worlds: this earth, the mid-world, and the divine. Therefore to meditate on the first measure of the mystic syllable, is to be busy with the things of earth alone, to have no hold at all on the two higher worlds.

To turn to the text: A question has been asked as to what world he gains, who meditates on the mystic syllable until the day of his death. The answer is, that the mystic syllable is a Symbol for the Eternal, the All.

That "he who meditates on the first measure only, vivified by it, is quickly reborn in the world of men." But "he who dwells on it in his mind with two measures, is led to the middle world.

He wins the lunar world, and, after enjoying brightness in the lunar world, he returns again, while he who, with three measures, meditates on the mystic syllable, and thereby reaches in meditation to the highest spirit, enters into the radiant, the divine sun.

As a serpent is freed from its slough, he verily is freed from the perishable. He beholds the indwelling spirit above the highest assemblage of lives." The first alternative is that of the "mean beings who are perpetually returning," who meditate only on things of this earth.

The two latter are, of course, the path of the fathers and the path of the gods, of which so much has been said already. The tract we have just quoted says of these: "They who follow ritual, thinking sacrifices and gifts are the perfect way, win the lunar world; they, verily return again.

This is the path of the fathers. But they who seek the Self by fervor, Service of the Eternal, faith and wisdom, these verily win the divine sun. This is the home of lives; this is the immortal, fearless, supreme way. From it they do not return again, for this is the perfect goal."

So we have traced the fate of souls, according to the luminous wisdom of the Upanishads, from the divine world downward into birth; then through life to death, from death upwards again through ethereal spheres to the divine world; thence again, when their spiritual energies are spent, downward through the ethereal world, through the gates of birth to this world again; for thus, verily, they go on along their cyclic course.

We have seen, further, how their ways diverge, according as divine or earthly energies hold sway, or are in equal balance. But, as it must be as rare for a soul to go forth with tendencies wholly earthward as it is for a soul to go forth with tendencies wholly heavenward, we must believe that, for the vast majority, there is the rest of paradise between death and birth; a long shining dream, where all the bright energies of their spirits work out their perfect fruition.

There is one problem that irresistibly presents itself, though perhaps it is hardly a profitable one: How long does the soul's rest in paradise last? How soon is the soul reborn?

One is led to imagine that there is a clue to this in a dark saying concerning the divine word in the Indian books—the word that became flesh and dwelt among us. We are told that a fourth part of the word is manifest on earth, while three fourths are invisible in the heavens.

May we take this to mean that the life-span in paradise is thrice as long as the life-span on earth, three times our earthly three-score years and ten? That our spiritual energies are thrice as potent as our earthly, and thus require thrice as long for their unfolding? This may be so, but we had better leave these high problems with the gods.

Only one thing remains to be said, to make this teaching complete. The paradise where the soul lingers between death and birth has been spoken of as a world of dream, where the spirit puts forth from itself joys, rejoicings and enjoyments, itself the magician, "having cut the wood itself, building itself."

We shall fail entirely of understanding, if we think that this earth, the world to which the soul returns, is of different texture, of other origin, than the world of paradise. Here too, in this world, the soul, the spirit, the immortal

Self is the only magician, weaving the worlds from his own self "as the web-wombed Spider weaves his web."

Both worlds are equally real, equally unreal. "He goes from death to death who sees a difference; what is here is, there also; what is there, the same is here." For here, as there, is the infinite Self only, the one and all: "the spirit that wakes in those that dream, molding desire after desire, is that bright one, that Eternal that they call the immortal one.

In this all the world rests, nor do any go beyond it. The one ruler, the inner Self of all beings, who makes one form manifold; the wise who behold him within themselves, theirs is happiness, not others. The durable among endurable; the soul of souls, who though one, disposes the desires of many; the wise who behold him within themselves, theirs is peace everlasting, and not others.

This is that, they think, the ineffable supreme joy. How then may I know whether this shines or borrows its light? No sun shines there, nor the moon and stars; nor lightning's, nor fire like this. All verily shines after that Shining; from the shining of that, all this borrows light."

THE BROAD MIND

It is becoming a virtue to be broadminded; but there are times when virtue becomes so virtuous that it ceases to contain any virtue. Likewise, it is possible for mind to become so broad that it no longer contains any breadth.

* * * *

To be progressive in thought is another admirable trait in the eyes of the modern world; but there are not a few of our advanced thinkers who advance so rapidly that their own minds are left behind. They become so absorbed in the act of moving forward that no attention is given to the power that alone can produce advancement. Consequently, their remarkable progress is in the imagination only.

* * * *

Not all is thought that comes from mind; and the mere fact that we are thinking does not prove that we are creating thought. Much of the average mind's product is but heaps of intellectual debris, gathered in one place today and in another tomorrow. Too much of our modern thinking is simply a moving of useless mental material through the various states of consciousness.

* * * *

Thought is the product of design, purpose and the working out of principles; and contains the power to serve certain definite objects in view. No product of mind is thought, unless it is the result of designed thinking, and is created for a certain special purpose. A pile of brick is not a house; but a house may be built from those bricks if they are arranged according to special design, and for a definite purpose.

* * * *

The broad mind should embrace much; but should not attempt to hold more than can be applied practically, thoroughly and according to the purpose of one's life. The object is not to see how much we can hold, but how much we can use; not how much ground we can cover, but how much we can cultivate scientifically.

* * * *

The mind that becomes broad enough to accept everything, will also accept the illusions, the vagaries and the foundationless theories that are so numerous everywhere. There are a number of people today who do this very thing, and call themselves liberal, advanced, charitable, and broadly progressive. The fact is, their minds are a hopeless mixture, and they accomplish nothing, and what is more serious, they confuse the beginners in the genuine advanced thought, and put to shame the real truths of all true progressive movements.

* * * *

There is a progress that is progressive; there is advancement that actually does advance, and we have much of it today; but there are many movements and many people claiming to be broad who are broad only in the sense of keeping the mental doors wide open to everything that may desire to come in. And the fact that such reckless broad-mindedness exists today to an enormous extent makes the subject serious, not only for the individual, but for the entire race.

* * * *

The mind that is broad in the true sense of the term does not try to embrace everything, but tries to penetrate everything. Its object is not to take in and hold; but to enter into, and understand.

* * * *

To be broad-minded is not to be ready to believe anything, but to be ready to examine everything. A broad mind never takes things on authority, but is eternally in search of the one authority—truth—that is back of and within all things. To be able to see the true side of every belief, every system, every idea, every experience—that is genuine broadmindedness.

* * * *

What we accept becomes a part of ourselves; therefore, to take in everything is one of the most serious mistakes that anyone can make. The fact is, we cannot exercise too much care in selecting our ideas; though we go to the other extreme when we become so particular that we are not satisfied with anything. There is a happy middle ground that everyone can establish by training the mind to penetrate everything for the purpose of understanding the principle that underlies all things.

* * * *

It has been well stated that we gradually grow into the likeness of that which we like; and it is true that we nearly always gain special admiration for that which we constantly defend, whether we have fully accepted the same as true, or not. The mind that is willing to accept almost anything for the sake of being broad, will be ready to defend almost anything to justify his position. Therefore, to defend all the theories that pass as advanced is to reproduce our minds in the likeness of all those theories; and since those theories contradict each other at almost every turn, the result will be a mind, divided against itself.

* * * *

A confused mind is the greatest obstacle to real progress; and the attempt to take in every new idea as true, because it is new, will confuse mind most sadly. And what is more, such a practice will so derange judgment, that after a while the mind will not be able to intelligently discriminate between the right and the wrong in any sphere of life.

* * * *

In this connection, it is well to remember ninety-nine percent of the new ideas that are sprung on the world are illusions; and the reason why so many of these ideas are accepted as true is because real broad-mindedness is an art yet to be acquired by people in general. The average mind is ready to take in and hold, if it happens to produce an impression favorable to his present condition of life; but there are few who are training their minds to penetrate everything for the purpose of understanding everything.

* * * *

The attitude of tolerance is usually considered an exceptional virtue; but again we are liable to be misled, because there are two kinds of tolerance. The one holds a passive charity for everything, without trying to find out the truth about anything; while the other enters into friendly relations with all things in order that the good and the true that may exist in those things can be found.

* * * *

The spirit of criticism never finds truth; but the spirit of friendly research always does. The penetrating mind must be kind, gentle and sympathetic; if it is not, the very elements that are to be examined will be scattered and misplaced. Besides, it is the substance of things that contains the truth; but to enter into this substance, mind must be in sympathetic touch with the life and the soul of that which it seeks to understand.

* * * *

The passive tolerance either is indifference or will soon become so; and mental indifference leads to mental stagnation; which in turn makes mind so negative that it is completely controlled by every condition or environment with which it may come in contact.

* * * *

True tolerance refrains from criticism at all times; but that is only one side of its nature; the other side enters into the closest mental contact with all things, and penetrates to the very depths of the principles upon which these things are based. In this way, mind readily discovers which ideas "and beliefs are true expressions of principles, and which ones are mere perversions. But the tolerant mind does not condemn the perversions; it forgets them entirely by giving added life and attention to the true expressions.

WHAT WE ALL WANT

Everybody is living for something, and is eternally trying to realize more and more of that something; but it is seldom perfectly clear what that something actually is.

Some expect to attain the heart's desire through the physical body, with its exterior functions and senses; others have selected the mind as the only path to the goal in view; while a limited number have resigned everything in the external that the soul may satisfy the longings of life.

Those who live for the body are criticized by those who live for the soul; and those who live principally for the mind, look with more or less pity upon the other two. All three, however, are living and working for the same thing. They all want life, and the good things that life can give; but their methods differ.

Those that live for the soul only, think themselves more holy than those who live for the body; and yet they are just as anxious for soul pleasure as the latter are for physical pleasure.

Therefore, if the one be wrong, the other must be wrong also; and likewise, if the one be holy, the other must be the same; for in the last analysis, pleasure is pleasure. Pleasure satisfies sense; but it cannot be any better, nor any worse to satisfy physical senses than spiritual senses.

True, there is a difference, but in degree only; and in this respect the one who lives for the soul is the gainer, because the spiritual senses, when satisfied, give far more pleasure than the physical ones. The different kinds of pleasure are produced by the same phase of consciousness acting upon various parts of the same scale of life; therefore, all who seek pleasure in its various forms, are seeking the one and the same thing.

We are all seeking pleasure; whether we expect to get it in this world or in some other world; we all desire pleasure, and we cannot deny it. Nor is it wrong to have such desires; but it is wrong to place limitations upon life by confusing the effects of pleasure with the causes. It is also wrong to mislead the lives of others by declaring that the pleasures that come through certain channels are unholy, while those that come through the ones out of reach are alone worthy of attention.

But if we should work only for the pleasures that are beyond us, and never permit ourselves to enjoy what is at hand, we should never enjoy anything, and to work for greater glories would be folly. Nevertheless, this is the philosophy that nine-tenths of the people in the world are being taught to follow.

It is not strange, therefore, that they are confused and do not know what they want, nor how to proceed to secure what they think they want. If it is right to seek the greater, it cannot be wrong to seek the lesser, so long as the person has not the capacity to comprehend and appreciate the greater. We find no fault with the child because it enjoys only that which is childish; neither should we find fault with those minds that have not yet learned to enjoy the pleasures of the soul.

The person who lives for the body usually does so because he does not know what else to live for. If he could understand a larger purpose in living, he would certainly accept it because we are created to seek both quantity and quality in everything.

The human mind has a natural tendency to desire the largest and the best, and it is only when we are in abnormal conditions that we remain satisfied with less than what we may now secure.

The person that lives for the body, wants life, the same as everybody else; and the physical form is the only channel to life that he has discovered. He therefore ought not to be found fault with for making the best use of the only instrument of life in his conscious possession.

Though the question is, if he is actually making the best use of what he does possess; but the same question may also be asked about those who live for the mind or the soul. The greatest problem in life is how to make the best use of everything that we have at hand now; and all the lesser problems are either parts of this greater one, or directly connected.

When we learn to make the best use of everything we now possess, we shall have found the secret of complete emancipation, and the path to perpetual attainment. All the ills in life come because we have not done our best; and the only way to climb to the greater heights is to go to the top of the mountain before us now.

From the top of every mountain in life there is a path that leads to the top of a still higher mountain; though there are too many who perpetually dream of the heights of the greater, but do nothing to reach the heights of the lesser.

These are not doing their best, no matter what they may be living for. They want life, but they do not wish to work up to life. They want a perfect heaven in that great day, but they do nothing to create heaven where they may be living in this lesser day.

The future is the result of the present; therefore, there is no future heaven in sight for those who do not try to make life a heaven now. This is a fact that is being realized more and more in this age; and in consequence, a great many methods for producing a present ideal life have been evolved.

But these methods do not all work for everybody; what works for one does not work for another, and this fact leads many to believe that all are wrong. They do not know, however, that all methods come from the same principle, and that no methods can produce permanent results unless the underlying principle is understood and applied.

Some minds find the principle through one method; other minds find the same principle through a different method. Therefore, all methods are good and necessary so long as they are employed only as methods; but when the method is looked upon as the secret, and the principle ignored, overlooked or forgotten, results are no longer produced.

Principles are promoted through good methods; but when the principle is ignored, the methods have nothing to promote; therefore, accomplish nothing. Sometimes methods, minus the principle, may appear to accomplish something; but they are simply taking the person around a circle by suggestion; removing one condition by taking consciousness into another that will soon prove to be just as limited and detrimental.

Every method suggests something; and every suggestion moves mind, changes thought, and thus temporarily relieves mind. But to move mind is one thing; to elevate mind is quite another. The latter can be produced only by the understanding of principles, and by using methods solely for the promotion of those principles. The living of life in its various phases, illustrates the same law. People want life, and use means to secure what they want; but too often they fall into the habit of seeking the means only, ignoring the real life that comes through the means.

People seek wealth fundamentally, because wealth can procure some of the good things of life; and they seek the good things of life because back of the good things is life itself—which is the very thing we all really want, whether we know it or not.

But too often mind becomes so delighted with the good things that life is forgotten; and later on is blinded by the glitter of wealth, and thus fails to see the goods things and their place in existence.

From this time on the mind seeks the wealth only; then it is that money becomes the root of all evil. It is loved for what it is, instead of what it can produce; and as it is of no value in itself, the mind that loves wealth for what it is only, turns attention upon the means instead of upon that which the means should produce.

The result is that the means are not employed, but hoarded; and mind becomes absorbed in lifeless things, thus losing consciousness of life itself.

Everything that can satisfy existence comes from life; therefore, when we lose consciousness of life, we fail to receive that which can satisfy, and unhappiness in its most disagreeable forms follow.

To be happy, seek life with heart and soul; use all available means to secure more life, but do not for one moment love life less than the means to life.

To use the physical senses as means to more life is perfectly legitimate; and there is nothing wrong in permitting the senses to enjoy the life that is expressed in their world; but when the physical senses are employed to gratify themselves for the sake of gratification, and not for the purpose of expressing more life, we come to the method without the principle; and the pleasure that appears for a season, ends in hollow mockery.

To use the mind or the soul to satisfy the longings of life, ends the same way, when the mental power or spiritual attainment are looked upon as ends in themselves. We must remember that all things are means to be used in the realization of more life, because it is life we all want.

Life alone can satisfy, fulfill and perfect life; therefore, life alone is the goal. All other things are to be consciously and intentionally used as means for reaching that goal. The mind that seeks spiritual states of consciousness simply because it is good to be there, will ere long seek those states of consciousness simply to satisfy his senses; and the end will be spiritual poverty with every high enjoyment taken away.

It is the ascension into life, and the expression of life that gives joy; but when we begin to seek the states of joy themselves, we no longer seek the life that produces those states. Therefore, those states will be produced no more, and we will be left empty-handed.

Millions today are in great spiritual hunger, because they have worshipped the forms and the letter that are supposed to represent spiritual life, and have ignored the spiritual life itself. They have depended upon the means, but have not sought the bread of life through the means. They have followed the belief, but have not sought the living faith and the absolute truth that constitute the soul of belief.

Millions today are mentally confused, because they have accepted methods, systems and formulated knowledge, but have not sought the principles that lie beneath. True, methods and systems are necessary; they are even indispensable, in all stages of development; but they are simply means through which the mind gains a larger and a larger consciousness of the real.

No one can become confused so long as he employs all methods to more fully understand principles, because in such an attitude his attention is concentrated upon principles, and will be held in poise, harmony, and security by principle.

To realize perfect peace of mind, and to attain constant enlargement of mind, direct attention always upon the principles that underlie all systems and forms of knowledge; and seek to understand those principles, ignoring the fact that the systems do not always perfectly represent the systems.

Systems are made by man, and are aids, subject to constant change; and they should be changed as the needs of the growing mind may require. But principles are uncreated, unchangeable and eternal; therefore, the mind that rests upon principles is always safe and secure. His house is built upon the rock, and can never be disturbed.

The spiritual hunger that is almost universal in this age can be entirely removed by using everything in life as means through which the life of the spirit can be realized; because just as soon as we begin to look beyond the form and the letter and the belief, and desire the living spirit itself, our hearts and souls will begin to receive those very things that we so long have yearned for, Whenever we place ourselves in touch with the inner life, the inner life awakens within us, and will express itself according to our desire and need; but it is not possible to realize the inner life so long as our minds are mixed up in forms, doctrines, beliefs, symbols and other empty shells. We must remember that life is the cause of everything that is necessary to the welfare and advancement of human existence, and that, fundamentally, it is life that we all want.

The more life we want, the truer we are to the truth upon which all life is based; and since all things that come from life are good, we are entitled to all the good things that life can give, whether they come through the use of the body, the mind or the soul. But to secure all that life can give, we must first secure life itself; and to secure life we must seek directly, constantly, and with the whole of our being.

Therefore, all means through which life may be secured should be fully employed; physical means, physical functions and physical senses included. The idea that real life can come only through mind and soul is not true. Real life can come through everything, and will come through everything that is intentionally employed as a means to life. But when we seek only the means, ignoring life, we are not seeking life.

When we are not seeking life we are not receiving life, but merely existing; and when we no longer receive life, we no longer receive anything else worth having. To seek the life more abundant through all things, is therefore the path to all that heart can wish for.

VIBRATIONS AND MENTAL IMAGERY

It has been discovered that geometrical figures, when imaged upon mind, regularly every day for a reasonable length of time, will develop intellect, reason, analysis, discrimination, and the power to understand basic principles.

It has also been discovered that every object, symbol or picture imaged upon mind affect the quality, the power and the capacity of the mind, and the various faculties and talents.

How great the effect is to be depends upon how deeply the nature of the mental image is felt, and how long it continues as a predominating picture; and what faculties are to be affected depends upon the form of the image.

From this fact it is evident that every faculty is directly related to a certain mental form, and that that form or image is directly related to a certain rate of vibration; because every form is a distinct expression, and every expression is the result of a certain rate of vibration.

To develop any faculty it is necessary to increase the volume of the vibration that is back of that faculty; and it is evident that this can be done when the real vibration back of the faculty is acted upon by consciousness while mind is conscious of an extra supply of creative energy.

But to reach the real vibration that is back of the faculty, we must cause mind to follow those lines of expression through which the real vibration comes forth into the faculty; and those lines of expression always combine into a distinct form.

Therefore, every faculty is the result of an abstract or mental form; and it is the reconstruction of this mental form on a larger scale that produces the larger faculty. The aggregation of all the mental forms produces the physical form; therefore, by changing certain mental forms we can modify the shape of the body, and improve physical appearance.

That the temperament of the person changes with the change of thought, and that a change in temperament produces a change in the personal appearance, are well-known facts; but the average person has not carried out this law as extensively as necessary to produce a clear-cut, decided demonstration.

However, the application of the law, whether to a slight degree or to a very great degree, proves that external form and shape are the effects of internal forms of thought. People who continue to live in the same mental groove, never change their appearance, unless it is to look a little older every year; and this change comes because they think they are growing older every year.

People who change their lines of thought, invariably change in physical appearance, either for good, or otherwise. When a person becomes absorbed in a narrow, mystical groove of thought, the physical body does not look so well, because the form of such thought is incomplete. When a person becomes absorbed in a narrow, materialistic groove, the form of thought is in the undeveloped state, and the body looks crude, ordinary, and undeveloped as a consequence.

The more perfect the form of the thought, the more in keeping are all the parts of the body, unless certain physical laws are violated to modify the natural results.

But perfect mental forms do not always produce a beautiful body; the reason being that there may be so many of one kind of mental forms, and so few of the others. The person who has only one strong talent is never handsome; and the above explains why. One-sided minds, however, are not necessary to great results along special lines, as so many suppose.

The genius who has one strong point, and is weak in every other respect, would become a greater genius if he made the other parts of his mentality almost as strong as his leading talent. People seem to think, however, that to develop the weaker parts of mind would take life and power away from the leading talent; they do not know that the average person wastes, through a lack of poise, enough energy to make all his talents as strong as the strongest one.

When all this power is saved and employed in the development of the whole mind, the leading talent will be backed up with a powerful mind, and can consequently accomplish far more than ever before. We therefore conclude that we have nothing to lose and everything to gain by ceasing to be one-sided.

To give every mental form the opportunity to stamp itself, in its most perfect and most developed state, upon the faculty and that part of the body to which it corresponds, should be the object; but to promote this object we must know the mental form of every mental faculty and every physical structure; and we must also know how to reconstruct that form on a larger and more perfect scale.

The latter is accomplished by gaining conscious control of the vibration that is back of and the cause of every mental form, and by changing that vibration according to the demands of the effect we desire to produce. As previously stated, geometrical figures correspond with the faculties of reason, analysis, discrimination and pure intelligence in general, though the effect of geometrical images upon mind is modified in accordance with what dimension predominates in the figure.

In the May issue it was stated that length corresponds with the physical, width with the metaphysical, and height with the spiritual; and in accordance with those facts it is evident that what part of man's being is to be effected by his mental forms depends upon which of the three dimensions is the most conspicuous to consciousness.

A figure where length predominates will arouse that part of intellect that can analyze objective, or physical things; and will intensify the growth of the body itself. The physical body in its last tangible analysis, is composed of fibers; and in all fibers the dimension of length is the most conspicuous.

Therefore, all mental images where the dimension of length predominates, will directly promote the health, the vitality, the stability as well as the orderly reconstruction of the body. A figure where width predominates will broaden the mind and arouse that part of intellect that can analyze thought and mental life in general. A more thorough understanding of metaphysics would inevitably follow the daily practice of imaging upon mind such geometrical figures that made the dimension of width the most conscious.

A figure where height predominates will elevate consciousness and increase the power of that part of intellect that can understand principles. Such mental images will produce a higher form of intellect; an intellect that can analyze the spiritual with the same accuracy that the more objective form of intellect can analyze elements, forces and things.

That an image or picture held in mind should have the power to arouse, stimulate and increase the power of these various forms of intellect may seem impossible, but when we understand how mental forms are related to the law of vibration—the power back of everything in the tangible universe—we shall discover the reason why these strange things are true; we shall also discover one of the greatest secrets in the world.

A geometrical figure where the circular predominates will, if imaged upon mind daily for some time, develop the power of comprehension; and a figure where the spherical predominates will develop in mind the power to see all things from all points of view. The reason for this is found in the fact that every mental picture or image is the unfoldment of an idea, and therefore expresses the nature of the idea.

A figure that is spherical is the unfoldment of an idea that contains the possibility of all points of view. If it did not, it could not unfold in every direction.

A figure that is circular is the unfoldment of an idea that contains the power to go around, to comprehend; therefore, when such ideas are unfolded in mind, the mind gains the power to go around things, because the nature and power of mind are the results of the ideas that have been and are being unfolded in mind.

Other geometrical figures exercise a molding power in mind for the same reason; they establish tendencies; and the creative powers—the powers that build faculties, talents, characteristics, qualities, etc.—follow the predominating tendencies. This is the law, and to take the fullest advantage of this law, so that we can get back of the entire formative process, is our object.

To illustrate; when we picture in mind a circular figure, or a perfect circle, we should not simply hold that image before mental vision, but should try to realize the idea—the circular idea—that is the center and source of the circular figure.

This we accomplish by turning attention to follow the circle of the circular figure, first at the circumference, then around a smaller circle, and a smaller circle within, until attention is actually in the innermost circular idea. When this is accomplished the mind does not view the mental picture of the circular figure, but realizes the idea of comprehension.

To bring about that realization every day through a mental exercise of a few minutes will remarkably develop the power of comprehension; but we are not to stop simply with the development of that mental faculty. When the idea of comprehension is realized, attention should be taken through that idea into the vibration that is at the foundation of the idea.

In other words, enter so perfectly into the feeling of the idea of comprehension, that you actually feel the vibrations that lie at the foundation. Then direct all the energies of mind through transmutation and concentration, upon that vibration; and the vibration that produces comprehension will be increased in power many times.

The result is that the power of comprehension will become so strong, and the faculty of comprehension so well developed that you can comprehend almost anything. If you are dull of comprehension, try this exercise for ten minutes every day, and in three months you will find improvements that will astonish yourself. When picturing any image upon mind, we should not simply try to hold that picture before the mental vision; but should try to get into the realization of the idea that is at the center of the picture.

When this is accomplished, we should try to feel the vibrations that produce the idea. Mere mental picturing produces decided effects upon mind, body, character, faculties, talents, etc., but to increase the effect of a desirable mental picture, we must increase the power of the vibration that produces the picture. This, however, modern metaphysics has not attempted to do; the reason being that no method was known through which we could gain control of the power back of thought.

But by tracing the channels of Form, Tone and Color back to the real vibrations from which they proceed, we enter into the presence of that power; and what we desire at the time, that power will fulfill. In this connection it is well to remember that in the ordinary mind all the tendencies are formed by the pictures that are constantly being impressed upon mind, because mind moves along the lines of these figures, and thereby forms tendencies; also, that every object that is seen by physical or mental sight produces an image upon mind, unless we consciously reject the impression.

We therefore see clearly why the mind becomes like its environments, or its imaginations, in the average person.

However, our object is not to permit every picture that appears, to become a formative power in mind, but to reconstruct out minds in the likeness of those superior images and ideals that we, through our own conscious efforts, choose to place before mental vision;

and also, to use those images as paths over which we may pass to the power—vibration—that is back of them all. Another fact of great importance, closely related to the subject under consideration, is that every abstract quality has a corresponding concrete form; and that that quality when expressed, appears through its corresponding form.

To bridge the gulf that seems to exist between the interior formless quality and its external form of expression has been attempted by nearly everybody, and in nearly every imaginable manner; but no results are secured until the mind is made to consciously touch the life of the inner quality.

This is readily accomplished by picturing the form of that quality upon mind, and then using that form as a bridge over which to cross the seeming gulf. The gulf does not exist in reality; it is only the inability of consciousness to grasp, or reach the inner quality that produces the seeming void.

But when the form of the quality is pictured in mind, and mind tries to follow the lines of that form to the center or idea within the form, the inner state desired is reached; and consciousness comes in contact with, and receives the quality it wished to realize and express. That this method will improve the quality of mind, or any part of mentality, is" well demonstrated among students of symbolism.

It is a well-known fact that an earnest study of symbolism with a view to understanding the inner meaning of the symbol, not only improves the quality of the mind, but improves remarkably the general condition of the intellect.

The reason for this is found in the fact that the person who tries to understand the inner meaning of a symbol, actually enters into the inner idea to a degree, and thus gains possession of the superior qualities of the inner mental depths.

But students of symbolism have not gained as much from their studies as they might; the reason being that they did not try to find the power back of the idea, and consequently did not increase the volume and capacity of that power by causing all the energies of mind to accumulate in that particular channel of expression.

This, however, they could have done by taking the mental process employed in their symbolical studies, and carrying it on just one or two degrees further into the depths of real mental life.

To understand how to employ symbolism in this w ay is extremely important, because nearly everything we come in contact with is more or less connected with symbolical phases of some kind; and what is more, every external form or object is the symbol of some internal idea.

By tracing the external form back to its corresponding idea, and then realizing or feeling the vibration that is back of the idea, the power back of all things is reached, and can be controlled and directed as we may desire. To find the idea that a symbol represents, we simply have to look for the predominating quality in the object or form. To illustrate, we will examine a spherical object that is pure white.

The white color represents completeness and purity, because in the white color all other colors are blended harmoniously; and purity always means completeness, order, and the proper expression of all the essentials to perfection in the sphere of action under consideration.

The idea back of the white color is therefore completeness, and by realizing the power back of the consciousness of this idea, and at the same time directing all the energies of the system into that state, we increase the power that is working for completeness in us; and consequently can perfect any part of the system into which we may direct the greater power.

As previously stated, the idea back of a spherical object contains the power to see things from all points of view; therefore, the predominating quality in a white spherical form would be completeness in every direction. To picture this symbol upon mind for a few moments every day, with a view to gaining consciousness of the power back of the predominating quality, will prove to be an exercise of extraordinary value. Make the image in mind a pure white globe, and try to draw the forces of mind from every part of the surface of the globe towards the center of the globe, holding the predominating quality—completeness in every way—constantly before attention. When attention gains the center of the globe, it should reverse its position so that instead of looking towards the center from every part of the surface, it stands at the center, and looks out towards every part of the surface. When this is accomplished, the mind actually feels completeness in every way, and realizes the idea of perfection in all things.

When this idea is realized, attention should pass through the idea into the power back of the idea, and enter the presence of the power that can produce completeness in every direction. While in the presence of this power, all the energies of the system should be drawn into the vibration of this power, and the power to perfect all things in the human system will be increased remarkably.

The power to see the perfect side of all things will also be developed; and there are few things that are more important. When the average person looks at ordinary physical light, he does not stop to think how that light represents Light in every sense of the term; therefore, does not use the light he sees to gain a consciousness of the greater light within.

This, however, should be done; and those who employ light in this way will steadily grow in superior wisdom. Turn attention upon the inner meaning of light, and try to realize or feel the power that is back of all light. When this realization is gained draw all the creative energies of the system into the vibration that is felt.

The result will be a decided increase of the power of wisdom and light in you. Since everything we see, represents an internal idea, in fact, is the expression of an internal idea, symbolism is an exact science; and when applied to its very foundation, is a science of the greatest value.

In this fullest application, all that is necessary is to picture the symbol upon the mind, find the predominant quality or central idea, cause the mental forces to follow the lines of the form of the symbol into the realization of the central idea, and then draw all the powers of mind into the feeling of the vibrations that are at the foundation of the idea.

The result is that the idea or quality represented by the symbol will develop in you. From the above brief description, symbolism and mental imagery gain new meanings, and prove themselves to contain unbounded possibilities. But to make the subject perfectly plain, and thoroughly practical, a number of illustrated articles will appear shortly.

THE LEADERS

He who seeks to become a leader must cultivate the ability to maintain at all times scrupulous reserve in regard to his own personal affairs. To parade before others one's own personal suffering and grievances, personal losses, and personal anxieties, is to lose their respect and confidence.

To parade before others one's own personal victories and achievements, one's personal advantages and opportunities, one's personal experiences in any way, is to lose power. The less one says about one's own personal life and interests, the more true self-respect and the more real power does one manifest.

The wisdom of sacred silence in regard to one's own life and one's own experiences cannot be too greatly emphasized. The quality of sacred reserve in regard to oneself is more or less natural with some people. Those to whom it is not natural can easily submit themselves to self-discipline in this respect. Such self-discipline necessitates first a clear vision of the ideal to be attained and a satisfactory reason for seeking to realize the ideal.

One must convince oneself that reserve and modesty are at once a mark of wisdom and an unquestionable index of power. When one is thoroughly convinced that reserve and sacred silence are admirable traits of character, it is comparatively an easy matter to establish them in one's life.

Again, it is of supreme importance that he who is pre paring to become a teacher or a leader in this work should exercise scrupulous silence and discretion in regard to his own training. Especially, should he remain silent in regard to the mission for which he is preparing himself.

Students will find it much to their advantage to exercise silence, reserve, and discretion even in their association with other students. There is meager reason why a student enrolled for private training should reveal to a fellow student the course of study he is pursuing or the lesson he is preparing. Yet, ever greater is the need of silence in regard to personal training in association with those who are not in sympathy with the work. The reserve one feels in regard to one's own study and progress should also be an incentive to reserve in regard to the study and the progress of others.

Therefore, an inner sense of the sacredness of each individual life should prompt every student to be re served and discreet in the questions he asks of other students. In a work of this nature, there is no place for curiosity and inquisitiveness.

Reserve and prudence in regard to giving information and in regard to seeking in formation of a personal nature mark the truly cultured man or woman. Silence in regard to training should include even more than one's own personal affairs. It should include all things that concern one's teacher. Nothing is more sacred than the communications between teacher and pupil, between Master and those who seek Mastership.

The student has a right to know that his communications, both verbal and written, are held absolutely sacred and confidential by his teacher. But it is equally important that the teacher is given as much reason to expect absolute sacredness and confidence on the part of the student. His communications and his instructions are individual and personal; and there is no occasion for repeating them to others. The mission of the Master is to lead the student to the Truth, and to guide him to the path of true development, and to help him find the Light within his own Center.

Loyalty to a teacher, or a guide, by no means puts one in bondage to an individuality, nor does it in any wise interfere with freedom of conscience and with exercise of personal judgment and opinion. Nor does it necessitate that follower and leader shall view all things through the same eyes. But it does demand a sweet-spirited reserve and deference.

The teacher interprets the laws of the Higher Kingdom to the student. In no detail does he interfere with personal freedom. In every way does he try to help the student to find his own Inner Guidance and his own Light and his own Center.

He tries to guide the student to the plane of Mastership over himself. The student gains confidence in his own Inner Guidance by following it according to his best understanding. Yet there are times when the severity of a teacher or the chiding of a Master are necessary stimulants to more earnest endeavor.

The follower who is not able to face his own conscience through the firm chiding of his guide is far from being qualified to enter upon leadership himself. The Master is far superior to the thought of personal following. He is far from asking for loyalty and support on the plane of personality. Ife is indifferent to personal praise and personal censure.

The admonition to the neophyte in regard to loyalty, reserve, and sacred silence concerning both training and Master comes from a source far removed from arbitrary man-made authority. The very nature of the relationship existing between neophyte and guide, the very conditions of soul growth, the very law of honesty and devotion, make it obligatory upon each to maintain the attitude of loyalty toward the other.

The admonition to cultivate reserve, silence, and discretion is applicable to everyone who seeks higher development. These qualities of character are of prime importance in the growth of every one. By Masters of all ages, the principles of silence in regard to personal matters, especially in regard to training, has been enjoined upon all who seek admittance into the Temple of Knowledge and Power. The reason for this becomes more and more apparent to the aspirant, the farther he advances on the path. He comes in time to see that the principle is indeed the secret of wisdom and power. It is in every sense to his own best interests to observe the law of silence and discretion.

Let it be emphasized in every possible way and from every possible point of view that the law of silence, reserve, and discretion has been through all ages enjoined upon neophytes because it is recognized as a condition of growth, just as the law of love and purity of heart is a condition of growth. Purity of heart opens up to one a clearer vision of truth. "Blessed are the pure in heart for they shall see God."

Silence and discretion are not enjoined upon others in any arbitrary sense nor through the power of external authority any more than purity of heart is enjoined through external authority. Experience proves that reserve, silence, and discretion are indeed cardinal virtues. While these qualities are recognized as features of true growth and therefore are enjoined upon all seekers after wisdom and power, yet it must be particularly emphasized that he who aspires to become a teacher or a leader must submit himself to the most rigid self-discipline in this respect.

He must exemplify in his personal life the power of discretion and reserve. A person often gives irresistible evidence of his faith in the power of truth, his faith in the power of the teachings he represents, by the fewness of his words in regard to it. An overabundance of words in regard to a system of teaching may indicate the feeling that it needs support or even apologies.

The power of a teacher or a leader is in direct proportion to his absolute faith in the truth advocated. The personal influence of a teacher is to be neither ignored nor despised; but it is to be particularly noted that the personal influence of a teacher is in direct proportion to the reserve and the silence he manifests in regard to personalities.

So important is it for the teacher or the leader to become thoroughly established in these cardinal virtues that he should be careful not to enter the field as a personal representative of the work "before the time is ripe."

In this, as in other things, often "haste makes waste." As an essential qualification for leadership and possibly the most difficult of attainment, it is absolutely necessary that the critical "I" should be transmuted into the "I" that can love, overlook, and forgive.

Nothing can retard the soul growth of the student more than the critical self, the self that finds fault with the habits of others, with the shortcomings of others, the self that is never satisfied, no matter how things are, simply because they are not according to the tastes of that particular exacting "I."

Not only does the spirit of criticism retard soul growth, but it becomes in the organism a most potent cause of ill-health to the body, and unrest to both mind and heart. In fact, the critical spirit is a poison that permeates the entire being and causes everything to be seen "as through a glass darkly."

If the organism is clogged with poisonous conditions, which cause all things to be seen "as through a glass darkly," it stands to reason that the judgment cannot be clear, the vision of a given situation cannot be accurate and trustworthy.

A pessimistic outlook is the natural result of such a condition of body, mind, and heart. Another individual of wholesome, sweet-spirited inclinations may view the same situation and find it pre-eminently encouraging. It is an easy matter to be at peace and in harmony with one's self when all things go well. In that ease, it does not require a student of the higher philosophy or a Master to feel satisfied; for anyone, even the most carnal and materialistic, can be satisfied and manifest sweetness of spirit when outer circumstances are to his liking.

When all things seem to be going wrong, when we are among those whose habits are different from ours, that is the time one must, through the inner harmony and peace, be at ease and at rest. One never knows true peace and harmony until he finds them within himself. To depend upon the inner harmony when external conditions and surroundings are not congenial, indicates true power and true attainment.

The critical personality invariably is out of harmony with itself. It is seeking in the externals of life and in other people that which can never be found except in its own inner consciousness. When it has found peace and harmony within, it will cease being annoyed by the inconsistencies and the inharmonies that attract its attention from outside.

Furthermore, that in another which annoys us, that in a given situation or condition which disturbs us, invariably is a reflection of some defect, some flaw, some error in our own nature. If we turn our attention to the rectifying of the error thus revealed in ourselves, we find that the external condition ceases to annoy.

The trait in another that irritates is to be accepted as a guide post, pointing clearly to the glaring needs of our own heart. If we sincerely seek the help of our own conscience in following the directions indicated by the guide, we soon become indifferent to the external cause of irritation.

Crudeness in manner of another which shocks or startles us invariably reveals a limitation in our own nature, and directs our attention to the need of "a deeper work of grace" in our own heart. We serve as the mirror of one another.

That which startles as well as that which calls forth admiration reflects a corresponding condition in the beholder. These are principles that must be thoroughly tested and applied in the lives of all who would attain self-knowledge and self-mastery. Especially must they he thoroughly mastered by him who aspires to become a teacher or a leader in the cause of truth and righteousness.

In the world are to be found all grades and strata of society, from the highest culture and education to the lowest depths of ignorance and superstition; from the most deli cate polish and refinement to the crudest possible expression of humanity; from professions that command millions and van the applause of men to the humble station of the one who barely earns his loaf of bread through menial service. We must expect nothing else than to find men and women who are stupid according to our standard, men and women who are unpolished and crude, men and women who are unappreciative and unresponsive. But he who complains of stupidity and who becomes irritated by crudeness and who is annoyed by lack of responsiveness has not yet reached the plane of leadership, and has much to overcome before he is able to lead others to peace of soul.

What of the soldier on march against the enemy? Even though he may have come from a home of refinement and luxury, does he in active service for his country expect all the comforts of life? Does he expect to be free from hard ship and toil and strain? Or does he not rather yield himself loyally and bravely to necessary conditions on equality with a comrade that may never have known what luxury is?

If carnal man, bent on the destruction of his fellow man, through loyalty to country and through love for the mission in which he is engaged, can forget the luxuries by which he was surrounded as a private citizen, and can enter heart and soul in his work, how much more should the soldier of the soul, he who helps men to find life instead of death, he willing to deny himself and to find peace and contentment in his great work? But so strangely is mankind constituted that, among those who seem, or at least who claim, to be highly evolved, are some who have developed a critical self far in advance of the most egotistical materialist.

It is sad that this should be so; nevertheless, it is true. And it is this critical self which must be mastered before man can become a leader of others and be a fit representative to show others “the way, the truth, and the life” that leads to peace, happiness, and immortality.

Soul Science and the Chirstic Interpretation, through the medium of the Temples of Illuminati and of Illumination, are gradually teaching mankind the way—not a new and untried way, but the way of the Masters and the Initiates of all centuries, a way tested and proved in the experience of many to be the way that leads to Mastership and to Illumination; the way that man must live in thought, word, and deed in order to become the creature God intended him to be.

As in other ages, when a cycle is completed and another is begun, there is a call for leaders who shall themselves first of all become imbued with the spirit and the principles of the Divine Law, and, through careful preparation, be qualified to carry to the multitudes the doctrine of Divine Unfoldment and Illumination. The center of instruction in Soul Science and the Chirstic Interpretation places no limitations on the qualification for leadership. Education and culture of a general nature are encouraged. Premiums are not offered to ignorance or to crudeness. None can be too highly cultured or too highly educated to take up leadership among the people. But dis crimination must be made between education that exaggerates the personality and education that develops character and true power; between culture of a narrow and artificial type and true culture of heart and soul.

A leader must be prepared to meet the common people, or the middle class of society, often designated as the working class. In order to do so successfully, he must possess true culture and refinement of heart. None are so keen to detect superficial culture as the man or the woman who is striving to live an unselfish life in service to others. In intercourse with the common people, the leader must be so highly cultured that he does not feel himself superior to them, he must not consider himself above them, nor hold himself beyond them. Even though he may strive to conceal it, if the feeling of superiority is present in his heart, it will be detected by the people and will repel rather than attract. If their ways and their idiosyncrasies are a shock to his temperament, it indicates that love has not yet perfected its work of purification in his own heart. Society in general is composed of strata, each of which considers itself superior to the one below.

Free America does not recognize clan and class distinction with such precision as do other countries; yet perhaps this very fact makes the social problem a delicate one. It is not uncommon for the colored man of the South to speak of the white man as "white trash." In like manner, there are those among the seemingly cultured of the white race who express contempt for their less fortunate brothers by calling them "low trash."

These expressions are here repeated with regret and sorrow of heart, merely to call attention to the chasm of separation that is felt between the different planes of the great human family, and to give an effective background to the statement that Soul Science and the Christic Interpretation stand for the Brotherhood of Man and for equality of souls. The difference in degree of culture and development between the colored man who calls the white man "trash" and the white man who speaks of a less fortunate brother of his own race in the same terms, is a difference of color only. In the case of the white man, it is an indication even of a less degree of culture for the reason that the white man has had greater opportunity, being free for centuries, whereas the colored man has but attained his legal freedom.

Let the Mystic or the one who would be a Mystic always hear in mind that in God's great universe there is no "trash," either white or colored. In the eyes of the All Father, the brother of lowly degree is as dear as is the man or woman of rarest culture. The lowest as well as the highest is on the path toward perfection. If there can be any difference, the great Father Heart has more regard and tenderness for the lowly brother because he needs more care and attention.

This thought is illustrated in the Christian hymn, "The Ninety and Nine," which voices a mighty truth. Let the one on the Mystic path always remember one thing: true culture is never manifested in criticism or condemnation; never in snobbery or scathing sarcasm; never in passing judgment nor in finding fault with the lowly; but forever and always is true culture manifested in giving the helping hand, with a heart full of love—a heart so full of love that the most humble of the humble may feel its radiations and be convinced of its genuineness.

You cannot call the faithful dog to you, at the same time holding a whip behind your hack and make believe that you wish to pet him; for instinctively he will feel the deceptive motive and turn away. Neither can you try to help the uneducated and the lowly and make them believe that you love them while cherishing in the heart a feeling of criticism, of judgment, or of superiority.

The principle of love and kindliness toward others does not encourage lowliness as such nor lack of external culture. Delicate refinement and polish of speech and manner are admirable indeed and much to be desired; but, unless they are accompanied by true refinement of heart and soul, they are to be classed as "paste and tinsel." It is also to be remembered that not uncommon is it to find a jewel of rarest value buried within the folds of an unattractive exterior.

Again, the principle of love and kindliness of heart to ward all does not advocate indiscriminate intercourse and familiar association between the different classes of society. Here again, the law of reserve and discretion will become one's guide. Love and kindliness in the heart will in time naturally find the happy medium, which bridges all chasms of separation and at the same time is careful not to violate the law of appropriateness, nor to infringe conspicuously on the tastes and the standards of possible onlookers. To the Soul of high and true culture, "all things are lawful, but not all things are expedient."

The principle of love and kindliness in the heart identifies itself with the attitude of indifference and with the spirit of non-resistance toward the actions of others. The one who aspires to become a representative of the Divine Law must discipline himself in the art of indifference and sweet non-resistance of spirit. The truly developed soul sees and hears many things without allowing them to make an impression on his mind. The act of seeing and hearing is accompanied by the act of "taking no notice;" consequently, it is the act of forgetting. It is possible to place oneself under such careful self-discipline that one becomes comparatively impervious to the acts and the characteristics of others, especially such acts and characteristics as tend to disturb or to shock or to annoy. This is an ideal greatly to be desired by all students of the higher philosophy.

Most of us at times are so situated that the affairs of others are seemingly thrust before our notice, giving opportunity for pronounced opinions in our mind regarding them. In order to maintain peace and harmony within our own hearts, thus enabling us to be at our best for the work that falls to our lot, it is wise to cultivate the art of attending strictly to our own business, the art of presenting the attitude of "holy indifference" and of "sweet non-resistance" toward the affairs of others. This attitude of mind toward matters that belong strictly to others in no wise stultifies the exercise of judgment and opinion in channels that demand our legitimate attention.

He who is preparing for leadership, even though his work as leader may be restricted to the most polished class of society, should be prepared in mind and heart to meet men and women in all walks of life, and to meet them with the feeling that there is no "gulf between." The student can accomplish nothing in the Inner Work theoretically, he must accomplish in actual realization, and receive the testing that comes through actual experience. Consequently, he who is consciously or unconsciously passing through the stages of preparation for leadership will doubtless be thrown into such circumstances in life as will fit him, in heart and in soul and in mind, to love, overlook, and forgive.

In every station of life there is demand for those who have attained kindliness of heart and an "excellent spirit." Remember, the young man Daniel was preferred above the presidents and the princes because an excellent spirit was in him." Let us pray that the Christ Flame—with its warmth of love, its light of understanding, and its chemic quality of a masterful will—may perfect its work of purification in our hearts and establish in our natures "an excellent spirit," and "a holy indifference and a sweet non-resistance to the actions of others."

It is a noteworthy fact that, in nearly every instance through all ages, the great leaders have been men who were reared in luxury and riches. Buddha, a prince of royal blood, a prince with such treasures at his command of silver, gold, and precious stones as would dazzle the eyes and the understanding even of the present-day millionaire, renounced all that he had and gave up his soul to meditation and study, and dedicated his life to teaching and helping the multitudes, the common people.

In Ancient Egypt, in the Temples of the Initiates, comparatively seldom did the sons and the daughters of the common people enter as neophytes, in order to become priests and vestals. It was more often the sons and the daughters of kings and princes that entered the temples and took the vows of the Priesthood, and gave themselves up to useful toil and to teaching the common people. And nowhere is there evidence that the common people appealed to the sons of priests and kings in vain; for the priest physicians and teachers and the vestal nurses were ever ready to help all who applied to them.

Even Moses, educated as he was in the temples among the priests, and learned in all the lore of the Egyptians, renounced all that was placed before him, in order to serve the common people. Instead of sleeping in a palace of marble and gold, for years he pillowed his head at night under trees in the wilderness.

The Master Jesus also, though born with a full heritage of innocence and refinement and power, though trained in the temples of the Masters, though possessing powers which might have given him all that heart could wish, renounced all and devoted his life in simplicity to teaching and healing the common people.

The supreme test is for a man to remain a gentleman, refined, and pure in heart and mind, even while he is serving the lowest of the lowly. This test brings the highest reward; and only he, in whose heart dwell pure love and devotion to mankind, can render such service. Nor must he who desires to serve God and humanity think that, in the humbler walks of life, a little learning, a little understanding, a little wisdom, will suffice. To be of the greatest service even among the lowest, a thorough understanding of the Divine Law is necessary.

Meager and superficial training in the principles of love, truth, and power may result in harm rather than in good. Let each individual who desires to prepare himself as a teacher, a leader, or a worker in the cause of truth and righteousness under the auspices of the Temple of Illumination place thoroughness of preparation before all else. Let him aspire to become truly and fully qualified. Let him haste not; but let him seek genuine, sincere, thorough "preparedness" of body, mind, heart, and soul.

Without the shadow of a doubt, the Chirstic Interpretation is the Power that is to lead the children of God, them that now dwell in ignorance, out of the wilderness of dark ness into the light of day; but, in order that the multitudes may come to understand the Word of God—the Divine Law—if is necessary for those who would lead them to understand the Word of God. This they can do in no other way than by giving up, like Buddha, Moses, and Jesus, their whole heart, mind, and soul to the service of the Master. To many, it may seem that this will require extreme self-denial, denial of things that make life worth living. In one sense, self-denial is called for; but in no other respect is self-denial demanded than in regard to things that are harmful either to the self or to others. Long past is the time when it was regarded a sin to smile on the Sabbath day. Long past is the time when it was considered wrong to meet in social converse. No longer is the social supper, the social game, and other recreations and sports to be classed among "mortal sins." We celebrate the cycle in which nothing is forbidden man which is not in itself harmful to the one indulging in it or to others.

All good things are ours to enjoy so long as our use of them harms neither the self nor others. Therefore, the leaders of men are to deny themselves only those things which are neither to their own good nor to the good of others. The leaders needed and wanted are men and women who have absolute faith in the system that they teach. They must understand the various aspects of the Divine Law and have a keen insight into its requirements.

They must understand that obedience to the Law is absolutely necessary in order that man may free himself from slavery to the carnal self, slavery to others, and consequent slavery to un-health, un-happiness, and misery.

Not only must the leader have supreme faith in the principles in the abstract, or theoretically considered; but he must have unwavering confidence in them as a power functioning in the lives of those to whom he ministers. He must have faith in “the Within” of each individual whom he serves. He must constantly keep his own will-power on the alert to enable him instantly to rise above doubt, suspicion, and surmising.

He must teach impersonally and impartially the principles of truth and righteousness, and the importance of thought control within oneself; but he must under no conditions sit in judgment over those who heed not his admonitions. What the teachings of Jesus were to humanity two thousand years ago will the Christic Interpretation be for humanity during the present cycle.

It makes clear the allegorical teachings of the Master, giving plain and definite instructions in regard to the attainment of Immortality of Soul, which is, in reality, Conscious At-one-ment with God, the Father, Creator of all things. The channels of instruction that represent the Christic Interpretation do not fasten arbitrary dogmas upon its adherents.

They state principles clearly and emphatically. These are essential as a foundation upon which to build. Adherents are not held by verbal vows or pledges. It is believed that the Christic teachings are of themselves all that is necessary whereby man may come into his divine heritage. Yet it is to be taken for granted that all who ally themselves with its ranks will be faithful to its teachings, to its organizations, and to its standards, and that all who benefit by its instructions will seek to bring others within its fold under the mantle of its protection.

If men and women could be made to see the future with its opportunities, they would come forward and prepare themselves, giving up heart and soul to the great work—a work that is not for the self alone, but for the self and for God and for humanity.

As in all things else, "preparedness" is the magic word. Unless man is thoroughly pre pared to do the thing he desires to do, he can scarcely hope for success. This is more than true in the great work of helping humanity to find the Center of Peace and Harmony within themselves. Unless man is prepared to meet in his own heart the conditions of the Divine

Law—the Law of Love and Forgiveness—in its varied aspects, he is liable to make many mistakes.

It is possible for one mistake to do more harm than can be remedied by doing a thousand good deeds thereafter. Strange to say, mankind is so constituted that it will forget a thousand things well done, while remembering the one mistake that attracted its attention. To become a leader demands an understanding of the needs of mankind as well as an understanding of the Divine Law.

Mankind generally is characterized by restlessness and uneasiness. Superficially considered, it may seem that this is due to self-seeking on the material plane, to a desire for things external, tangible, and visible, as a source of happiness. It must be admitted that there is an artificial unrest that seeks satisfaction on the plane of externals; but, on looking deeper, there is every reason to believe that the cause is beneath the surface, and that there is a general hunger for that which satisfies the soul.

Not understanding exactly what it is for which they hunger, men are turning hither and thither in search of something to satisfy their craving and unrest. Not knowing where and how to direct their search, they look without, vainly hoping to find peace and happiness in material splendor and temporal power. Thus, appearances indicate that men are becoming more and. more material in their tendencies, and less and less spiritual. Whereas, this very unrest in regard to externals indicates a deeper hunger and yearning.

Never in the history of the world did men seek more for the things that satisfy the soul than at the present time. The unrest that characterizes humanity at the present time is so deep and so mighty that it threatens to sweep all before it unless relief is found, unless there is a new foundation on which to build the future civilization.

This foundation is to be found in the Divine Law and the Christic Interpretation of the teachings of the great Masters—an interpretation that makes the teachings practical in their application to the needs of everyday life; an interpretation that will enable man to attain peace, happiness, health, and success, and to inaugurate a new and glorious civilization, which shall stand as a practical illustration of the Brother hood of Man.

Never before in the history of the world were there greater opportunities for the young man and woman, for the minister of the Gospel, for leaders in churches. A work of this nature, in the beginning at least, calls for courage, as does any work that has not the universal approval of mankind; but people who have the welfare of humanity at heart care not for the approval of men. Bear in mind that no one can truly serve God and humanity unless he is willing to do this regardless of the favor of men. Those who serve thus ungrudgingly are the ones who have been canonized as Saints.

But, after all, even though the honor comes not to man in this life, the satisfaction that he has done his best, that he has followed the dictates of his own heart and conscience, is sufficient reward for all suffering that may fall to his lot.

The time is ripe for the Divine Law and the Christic Interpretation to be presented to the people. Men and women who are duly and truly prepared are needed to go forward and spread the Soul Illumining Gospel and the

Science of Soul that directs the Way to Immortality.

QUESTIONS AND ANSWERS

In what sense is the Ruler of this Planet our Father? Is he: [a] our Creator; or, [b] our loving Guide and Guardian?

The Planetary Ruler, as I understand from those much wiser than I, is in no sense a "Creator". He sustains a relation somewhat analogous to that of a ruler of an absolute monarchy; except of an immeasurably more exalted and perfect character, and his "kingdom" is a spiritual one, and includes the entire Planet and all its planes and conditions.

If there is a divine element somehow present in mineral, vegetable, animal and man, is it an emanation from the Father? Would this be the probable meaning of the statement attributed to St. Paul, that God is not far from every one of us; for "in Him we live and move and have our being."

Before I could give even a fair guess at the answer to your second general question, I should have to know exactly what you mean by "divine". It is stated in substance, however, that the four kingdoms of Nature—Mineral, Vegetable, Animal and Human—are governed by the four "Life Elements". These "Life Elements", in their evolutionary order, are "Electro-Magnetic","Vito-Chemical", "Spiritual" and "Soul". - In the Mineral Kingdom is but one—the Electro-Magnetic. In the Vegetable there are two, of which the Vito-Chemical is the dominant one. In the Animal there are three, of which the Spiritual is the highest and dominant one. In the Human there are four, of which the Soul Element is the highest and the dominant.

Nowhere, however, are these Life Elements referred to as "Divine". Natural Science finds that these Life Elements are universal in time and space; and if they are looked upon as being "manifestations of the Great Universal Intelligence" which also is conceived to be universal in time and space—then I can understand how they might be spoken of as "Divine", or a "Part of the Divine", or as "Manifestations of the Divine", etc. It is possible that Paul may have had some such concept of "Divinity". The quotation to which you refer would seem to bear that construction.

Christ is reported to have said that God marks the fall even of a sparrow [Matt. 10, 29] and numbered the very hairs of our heads. Does the Father, then, personally know and watch each one of us, and hear our cries for help in a just Cause? If this is so, what need is there for the Great Friends as Messengers of one already with us, or auxiliaries of an All-Wise and Omnipotent Helper?

From this it is clear that "The Great Friends" and the "Spiritual Helpers" do really hear our cries for help, and do answer them as far as they can when they deem our prayers just and find us in real need of the help for which we ask. But even the Beloved Master does not presume to say that all the agencies that answer prayers may not be merely the 'Messengers" of the "Great Universal Intelligence". He frankly says "We do not know".

FINIS

For those interested in Rosicrucian or similar esoteric teaching.

Soul.org
Theosophical.org
WhitEagleLodge.org
PTTHfoundation.com

www.ingramcontent.com/pod-product-compliance
Ingram Content Group UK Ltd.
Pitfield, Milton Keynes, MK11 3LW, UK
UKHW020222250726
13967UKWH00001B/146

9 780359 143375